CENTRAL FLORENCE

Numbered spots on the map relate to pictured sights

Museo Botanico

San Marco

Giardino dei Semplici

Palazzo Pandolfini

Palazzo Medíceo

Palazzo Capponi

Giardino della Gherardesca

Cimitero della Misericordia

Università

Santissima Annunziata

Galleria dell'Accademia

Palazzo Gerini

Ferdinando I

Ospedale d Innocenti

Cimitero degli Inglesi

Mostre di Leonardo

Palazzo Pucci

Museo Archeologico

Palazzo Paneiatichi Ximenes

Piazza Massimo D'Azeglio

Ospedale S Maria Nuova

Museo dell'Opera del Duomo

Teatro d Pergola

Santa Maria Maddalena dei Pazzi

Crocifisso d Perugina

Museo di Firenze com'era

Volta di S Piero

Sinagoga

Museo ale di ologia logia

Casa di Dante

Palazzo Alessandri

Palazzo Pandolfini

Palazzo Borghese

Bargello

Badia Florentina

Teatro G Verdi

Casa Buonarroti

San Firenze

Palazzo Vecchio

Piazza Santa Croce Casa d'Antella

Santa Croce

Piazza Cesare Beccaria

Porta alla Croce

ACI

di Storia Scienza

Palazzo Vita

Biblioteca Nazionale

Museo Horne

Cappella dei Pazzi
S CROCE

Torre d Zecca

Piazza Plave

Ponte alle Grazie

LUNGARNO D GRAZIE

LUNG D ZECCA VECCHIA

LUNG PECORI GIRALDI

Palazzo Serristori

PONTE S NICCOLÒ

Ch Tedesco

Museo Bardini

Palazzo de Mozzi

Porta San Niccolò

SAN NICCOLÒ

Piazza G Poggi

Camping Michelangelo

Piazza Francesco Ferrucci

David

Piazzale Michelangelo

San Salvatore al Monte

Convento d Stimmatine

San Miniato al Monte

Cimitero delle Porte Sante

0   200 m

0   200 yds

Fodor's

Florence's 25Best

by Susannah Perry

Fodor's Travel Publications
New York • Toronto •
London • Sydney • Auckland
www.fodors.com

How to Use This Book

KEY TO SYMBOLS

➕ Map reference to the accompanying fold–out map

✉ Address

☎ Telephone number

🕐 Opening/closing times

🍴 Restaurant or café

🚆 Nearest rail station

Ⓜ Nearest subway (Metro) station

🚌 Nearest bus route

⛴ Nearest riverboat or ferry stop

♿ Facilities for visitors with disabilities

❓ Other practical information

▷ Further information

ℹ Tourist information

✋ Admission charges: Expensive (over €5), Moderate (€3–5), and Inexpensive (€3 or less)

★ Major Sight   ★ Minor Sight

👣 Walks   🚐 Excursions

🏠 Shops

🎵 Entertainment and Nightlife

🍽 Restaurants

This guide is divided into four sections

• Essential Florence: an introduction to the city and tips on making the most of your stay.

• Florence by Area: We've broken the city into four areas, and recommended the best sights, shops, entertainment venues, nightlife and restaurants in each one. Suggested walks help you to explore on foot.

• Where to Stay: the best hotels, whether you're looking for luxury, budget or something in between.

• Need to Know: the info you need to make your trip run smoothly, including getting about by public transport, weather tips, emergency phone numbers and useful websites.

Navigation In the Florence by Area chapter, we've given each area its own colour, which is also used on the locator maps throughout the book and the map on the inside front cover.

Maps The fold–out map accompanying this book is a compre-hensive street plan of Florence. The grid on this fold–out map is the same as the grid on the locator maps within the book. We've given grid references within the book for each sight and listing.

Contents

CONTENTS

Introducing Florence

Florence, the Cradle of the Renaissance: This little city contributes so much to European culture through its paintings, harmonious *palazzi* that line the narrow streets, monumental civic buildings and splendid churches dominating spacious piazzas.

Getting around is easy. The core of the city is tiny and you can walk nearly everywhere, made more pleasant with the pedestrianization of the area from the Duomo south through Piazza della Signoria to the Ponte Vecchio and east from the Signoria to Santa Croce. However, the sheer number of tourists during peak times can make walking painfully slow. Yet the Florentines have no intention of killing the goose that lays the golden egg, and have poured money into doing whatever's possible to make the city visitor-friendly. Prices are high, but not too high. Hotels and restaurants provide what their customers want; museums have been revamped wherever possible; and shopping is taken seriously—after all, this is Italy.

Florence should be a pleasure, not a cultural marathon. Try to concentrate on what you want to do, not what you think you should do.

You might find more pleasure in exploring the quiet streets of the Oltrarno, crammed with little workshops, than standing in line for hours to jostle for two minutes in front of a Botticelli masterpiece. A leisurely picnic in the green oasis of the Boboli Gardens may be more memorable than an overpriced pizza in a crowded bar. If you do want to saturate yourself with Renaissance art, plan ahead and reserve tickets.

Close to the city lies some of Italy's most beautiful countryside, a dreamy landscape of rolling hills dotted with villages and solitary cypresses. Even though every year sees a rise in visitors, the heart of Florence retains the richness of its golden age and little has changed since the great construction works of the Renaissance. But it's up to you to get beneath the bewilderingly crowded surface of Florence to the beautiful heart underneath.

Facts + Figures

- Florence attracts around 6 million visitors a year.
- The native population is around 370,000.
- Florencence has one of the lowest birth rates in Italy.
- The Uffizi Gallery is Italy's most visited museum—some 1.5 million a year.

UFFIZI BOMBING

In May 1993 a huge bomb exploded on the west side of the Uffizi, killing five people, causing structural harm to the building, destroying the Gregoriophilus Library and damaging some 32 pictures, three of which were totally destroyed. Once thought to have been the work of the Mafia, the crime remains unsolved and the culprits have never been caught.

ON THE BALL

The Medici family, virtual sovereigns from the 14th to 18th centuries, left their mark on every building owned by or connected with them, so look out for their coat of arms, a varying number of balls (*palle*) on a shield, on buildings everywhere. The *palle* probably represent pills or coins, references to their original trade as apothecaries and later role as bankers.

FLOOD FACTS

In November 1966 the River Arno burst its banks to disastrous effect: The tide, bludgeoning through the streets reached as high as 6m (20ft) in the Santa Croce region. This was not the only flood there has ever been, however: Bridges were swept away in 1269 and 1333, and the city was submerged in 1557 and 1884, but not as badly as in 1966.

A Short Stay in Florence

DAY 1

Morning Make an early start and head to the **Duomo** (▷ 58–59) to gaze on its mighty proportions; alongside are the superb **Campanile** (▷ 56) and **Battistero** (▷ 55). You can find out more about the history at the nearby **Museo dell'Opera del Duomo** (▷ 62). If you are feeling fit climb to the top of either the Duomo or Campanile for great views of the city but remember you will probably be jostling for space.

Mid-morning Take a coffee at one of the café-terraces along the traffic-free Piazza del Duomo to recharge your batteries. Head northwest up to the **Mercato Centrale** (▷ 68) at San Lorenzo—it is only open until 2pm—and check out the amazing fresh produce. You can then browse the leather stalls of the **Mercato San Lorenzo** (▷ 68)—keep a look out for pickpockets, make sure you're buying a bargain and don't be afraid to haggle.

Lunch Right by the market is the unassuming **Gozzi Sergio** (▷ 75), renowned for its hearty Tuscan fare.

Afternoon Finish your shopping and then walk down Via Pucci and right into Via Ricasoli—or take bus 1, 6 or 17—to the **Galleria dell'Accademia** (▷ 60–61) to view Michelangelo's massive masterpiece *David*. There's plenty more to see in the gallery or you may prefer to visit nearby **San Marco** (▷ 65) before returning to your hotel.

Dinner For a special treat try **Hosteria Bibendum** (▷ 49) in the **Hotel Helvetia & Bristol** in Via de'Pesconi (▷ 112). For a cheaper option there's **Belle Donne** (▷ 47), located close to **Via de' Tornabuoni** (▷ 36).

Evening Stroll down to the grandiose **Piazza della Repubblica** (▷ 39) with its triumphal arch, for a touch of Florentine atmosphere.

DAY 2

Morning Lines form as early as 7am at the **Galleria degli Uffizi** (▷ 30–31), with its priceless paintings and sculptures, so get there as early as you can; be patient and you will be rewarded.

Mid-morning Just behind the Uffizi, relax with a coffee at **Rivoire** (▷ 50) the best and probably the most expensive café in **Piazza della Signoria** (▷ 28). Leave the piazza and turn left into Via Por Santa Maria and stroll over the **Ponte Vecchio** (▷ 34–35) to be dazzled by its jewellery shops. There are plenty more gift shops just over the bridge.

Lunch Grab a light lunch at the **Café Pitti** (▷ 91) opposite the entrance of the Palazzo Pitti.

Afternoon Take in the Palazzo Pitti (▷ 84–85). There are four museums, plus the Royal Apartments to see, or if the weather is hot you might rather stroll in the **Boboli Gardens** (▷ 82). Be prepared for crowds. Then wander around the streets of Oltrano and along to the church of Santa Maria del Carmine with its wonderful frescoes. This area has workshops, local stores and cafés. If you are feeling fit cross back over the bridge and walk along the riverfront down to **Santa Croce** (▷ 29).

Dinner The Boccadama (▷ 47) wine bar-cum-restaurant is in a nice spot to appreciate the lively square of Santa Croce.

Evening If the weather is kind you can get a great view of the city after dark from **Piazzale Michelangelo** (▷ 87) in the southeast of Oltrano. Catch bus 13 to get there. Alternatively, take bus 7 up to the hill town of **Fiesole** (▷ 98) for wonderful views of Florence illuminated at night.

Top 25

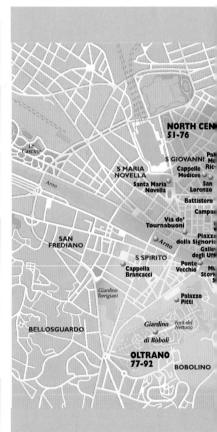

▶▶▶

Bargello ▷ 24–25
Overview of Florentine sculpture through works by Michelangelo, and others.

Battistero ▷ 55 One of Florence's oldest buildings, famous for its three sets of bronze doors.

Campanile ▷ 56 An incredible sight towering 85m (278ft) over the city.

Via de' Tornabuoni ▷ 36
The cream of world fashion elegantly displayed in the heart of Medieval Florence.

Santissima Annunziata
▷ 67 Elegant, neoclassical arches grace the façade of this lovely church.

Santa Croce ▷ 29 The largest Franciscan church in Italy incorporating the Cappella dei Pazzi.

Santa Maria Novella
▷ 66 A great Florentine church full of superb artworks.

San Miniato al Monte
▷ 83 A fine Romanesque church perched on a hill with wonderful views.

San Marco ▷ 65
Beautiful convent where the paintings of Fra Angelico are a feast for the eyes.

San Lorenzo ▷ 64 This church is a superb example of archetypal Renaissance architecture.

Ponte Vecchio ▷ 34–35
One of the immediately recognisable emblems of Florence.

Piazza della Signoria
▷ 28 A traffic-free sculpture gallery with elegant cafés and restaurants.

These pages are a quick guide to the Top 25, which are described in more detail later. Here they are listed alphabetically and the tinted background shows the area they are in.

Capella Brancacci ▷ 81
The chapel is covered from top to bottom with a monumental fresco cycle.

Cappella dei Pazzi ▷ 26
An early Renaissance masterpiece by Filippo Brunelleschi.

Cappelle Medicee ▷ 57
The Medici family's private chapels, visable proof of the dynasty's wealth.

Duomo ▷ 58–59 A sublime masterpiece of Renaissance architecture with a mighty dome.

Galleria degli Uffizi ▷ 30–31 One of Europe's oldest and best galleries to view Renaissance art.

Galleria dell'Accademia ▷ 60–61 Home to *David*, Michelangelo's world-famous sculpture.

Giardino di Boboli ▷ 82 A green space in the middle of Florence, a cool oasis on a hot summer's day.

Museo dell'Opera del Duomo ▷ 62 Home to the Duomo collection.

Museo Stibbert ▷ 97 An interactive exhibition of historic weaponry and military costume.

Museo di Storia della Scienza ▷ 27 The history of science brought to life with this fine collection.

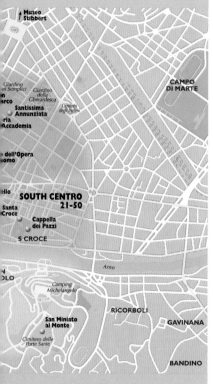

Palazzo Vecchio ▷ 32
The grand embodiment of Florentine civic purposes from the 14th century.

Palazzo Pitti ▷ 84–85
The city's largest and most opulent palace containing a fine picture collection.

Palazzo Medici-Riccaradi ▷ 63 A massive palace, the residence of the Medici until 1540.

◄ ◄ ◄

Shopping

Florence is high on every foreign shopper's itinerary, but it's also a big attraction for Italians, who rate it highly for leather goods, fabrics, bed linens, lingerie, china and ceramics. As Tuscany's capital, Florence has the pick of Tuscan goods and shops, and people come from all over the region for a wider choice than they'll find at home. In the era of the global market, much of what's on sale is available worldwide, but the choice is wider and the prices often lower for many Italian essentials. Designer fashion also draws the crowds; one of Florence's many claims to fame is as the headquarters of Gucci.

Something to Take Home

The nicest souvenirs are often everyday items—kitchenware, household linens, tools and quirky stationery. Head for the markets for good value espresso coffeemakers and the tiny cups to go with them, wonderful gadgets such as fish-scalers and plastic goods in vivid shades. Fresh produce and leather goods are also in plentiful supply in Florence's markets. Plastic also features heavily in the inexpensive and cheerful children's toys; best values are often in tiny shops away from the main streets. Food is a popular take-home; you could consider more prosaic goods than expensive oils

---

STREET TRADE

Street trading is an essential part of the Florentine scene, with tourists being offered everything from fake designer bags to lighters and African artefacts. Some traders are unlicensed and keep a constant eye open for approaching *carabinieri*, ready to scoop up their merchandise and run. Unless you want to buy, don't stop and look; if you do, you'll be a prime target, engaged on a protracted haggle that should get the price down by about two thirds. A number of traders are from North Africa and Senegal, often students or graduates who aim to make enough money in a few years in Italy to secure their financial future at home.

Florence is the place to shop for shoes, designer names, culinary delights, and, of course, ice cream

and wine—how about herb packs specially blended for different foods, the excellent stock cubes known as *dadi* or sachets of vanilla sugar?

Traditional Crafts

One of Florence's major attractions is the wealth of artisan workshops, clustered mainly across the river in the Oltrano area. Many specialize in antiques restoration for the city's numerous dealers, but there's more. Look for picture framers where you can get new purchases mounted, shoemakers selling wonderful velvet pads and brushes and marble-paper makers where you may have a chance to watch the whole creative process.

Florence on View

Prints, books and old maps and city plans make special souvenirs, and there are cookbooks on Tuscan cuisine, many in English. Beautiful calendars with views of Florence are on sale as early as April for the following year. The museum shops are good for these too.

Florentine Kitsch

There's no chance that you'll be overwhelmed by good taste either; there are T-shirts bearing images of Michelangelo and Botticelli, plastic models of the Duomo and Ponte Vecchio, umbrellas shaped like the Duomo, grotesque ceramics and fakes of every description. Where else could you buy such a blatant silvery reproduction of Michelangelo's David, complete with twinkling lights?

Something to take home—a bag from the market, herbs, or a fashionable accessory from a top Florentine name

---

ON A BUDGET

Markets are the best source of inexpensive and second-hand clothing with an Italian twist. The weekly Cascine market (▷ 98) is where the Florentines go for bargains—dive into the most crowded stalls. The area around San Lorenzo is good trawling ground for up-to-the-minute, inexpensive and cheerful designs. The Mall, a 30-minute drive south of Florence at Leccio, has outlets for Gucci, Armani and other leading brands.

Shopping by Theme

For a more detailed write-up of these shops, see Florence by Area.

ANTIQUES/PRINTS

Antichità Chelina (▷ 89)
Antichità Monna Angese (▷ 102)
Baccani (▷ 41)
Bartolozzi & Maioli (▷ 89)
Bottega delle Stampe (▷ 89)
La Casa della Stampa (▷ 89)
Ducci (▷ 41)
Giovanni Turchi (▷ 90)
Vanda Nencioni (▷ 44)

CERAMICS/PORCELAIN

Armando Poggi (▷ 41)
Arte Creta (▷ 71)
Bartolini (▷ 71)
La Botteghina (▷ 71)
Carioloa (▷ 101)
Carnesecchi (▷ 89)
Cermiche Artishiche (▷ 102)
Ceramisti d'Art (▷ 101)
Cose del Passato (▷ 41)
Diss (▷ 89)
Emporium (▷ 72)
Lenzi Ghino Giacomo (▷ 101)
Pampaloni (▷ 43)
Richard Ginori (▷ 73)
Sgiboli Terracotte (▷ 73)

FASHION

Angela Caputi (▷ 41)
Anna (▷ 89)
Balloon (▷ 71)
Coin (▷ 41)
Cortecci Abbigliamento (▷ 102)
Echo (▷ 71)
Emilio Cavallini (▷ 41)
Emilio Pucci (▷ 42)
Gucci (▷ 42)
Hermès (▷ 72)
Intimissimi (▷ 72)
Luisa (▷ 42)

Max & Co (▷ 43)
Maxmara (▷ 72)
Pitti Casmere (▷ 90)
Prada (▷ 43)
Principe (▷ 43)
Quelle Tre (▷ 73)
La Rinascente (▷ 44)
Roberto Cavalli (▷ 44)
Tessutia Mano (▷ 102)
Sisley (▷ 44)
Zini (▷ 73)

GOLD/JEWELLERY

Alcozer & J (▷ 89)
Bottega Orafa Penko (▷ 71)
Bvlgari (▷ 41)
Fratelli Piccini (▷ 42)
The Gold Corner (▷ 42)
Gualtieri Gandolfi (▷ 42)
Ore Due (▷ 43)
Ornamenta (▷ 72)
Paolo Capri (▷ 101)
Parenti (▷ 43)
Pianegonda (▷ 43)

LEATHER/SHOES

Il Bosonte (▷ 41)
Cellerini (▷ 41)
Francesco (▷ 90)
Fratelli Rossetti (▷ 42)
Furla (▷ 42)
Leather School (▷ 42)
Madova Gloves (▷ 90)
Martelli (▷ 42)
Misuri (▷ 43)
Romano (▷ 44)
Salvatore Ferragamo (▷ 44)

LINEN/FABRICS

Antico Setificio Fiorentino (▷ 89)
Città di San Gallo (▷ 41)

Ermeni (▷ 72)
Frette (▷ 72)
Loretta Caponi (▷ 72)
Passamaneria Toscana (▷ 73)
Siena Ricama (▷ 102)
Valli (▷ 44)
Valmar (▷ 44)
Abacus (▷ 71)

STATIONERY/GIFTS

Alice's Masks Art Studio (▷ 71)
Bottega del Mosaico (▷ 89)
Fratelli Alinari (▷ 72)
Giulio Giannini e Figlio (▷ 90)
Moleria Locchi (▷ 90)
Paper Exchange (▷ 72)
Il Papiro (▷ 73)
Parione (▷ 43)
Le Pietre Nell'Arte (▷ 73)
Pineider (▷ 43)
Scriptorium (▷ 73)
Sorbi (▷ 44)
Il Torchio (▷ 90)

WINE/FOOD

La Bogetta della Frutta (▷ 41)
Borgo (▷ 71)
La Cacioteca (▷ 101)
Café do Brasil (▷ 71)
Casa del Vino (▷ 71)
Drogheria Manganelli (▷ 102)
Federico Salza (▷ 101)
Marino (▷ 90)
Marsili Constantino (▷ 101)
Morbidi (▷ 102)
Olio & Convivium (▷ 90)
Paolo Peri (▷ 90)
Il Pasani (▷ 101)
Pegna (▷ 43)
Il Sapori del Chianti (▷ 72)
Vinarius (▷ 44)
Zanobini (▷ 73)

Florence by Night

To kick off your evening and for a taste of local life don't miss the *passeggiata*. Year-round, this quintessentially Italian nightly ritual sees the streets thronged with hundreds of locals, out to see and be seen, while window-shopping and meeting friends.

An Evening Stroll
The best place to see the fashion peacocks in their finery is on Via dei Calzaiuoli, linking Piazza del Duomo with Piazza della Signoria. To enjoy a drink while you people-watch, go to Piazza della Repubblica, with its expensive cafés. After dinner, wander along the Lungarni, the name given to the streets beside the river. The Ponte Vecchio is just as crowded by night as by day.

Stunning by night
Evening is the ideal time to admire Florentine architecture as the floodlighting enhances many buildings. Don't miss the Piazza della Signoria and the area between it and the Duomo. The private *palazzi* look superb at this time of day and you can peek into courtyards and loggias. Street entertainers add to the atmosphere.

Culture, Concerts and Clubbing
Florence has a year-round schedule of cultural evening events. The free monthly tourist magazine *Chiavi d'Oro* Toscana has full listings. Newspapers are another good source. *Firenze Spettacolo* also details everything that's on including rock concerts, clubs and discos.

A night out? Choose from a walk by the river, a concert in a church, or a drink in one of the city's historic bars

---

PICK OF THE PANORAMAS

A great evening vantage point is Piazzale Michelangelo (▷ 87), which gives a glorious panorama of the Duomo illuminated, Florence's twinkling lights and the misty hills beyond. The square draws the crowds during the day but things are quieter at night. There's a restaurant and a couple of bars if you want to spend the evening here; avoid the park/gardens area below the square at night. In late June, the square hosts the spectacular firework display celebrating the feast of San Giovanni.

Eating Out

Eating is definitely one of life's pleasures in Florence, as it is all over Italy. The food is fresh, seasonal and, above all, local. You'll eat the best of Tuscan produce cooked to Tuscan recipes.

Mealtimes
If you are heading for breakfast in a bar, most open for business around 7–7.30. Restaurants normally open for lunch around 12.30 or 1 and stop serving at 3; they close for the afternoon and reopen for dinner around 7.30–8. All restaurants have one closing day a week, but many places open every day in summer.

Where to Eat
Trattorie are usually family-run places and are generally more basic than restaurants. Sometimes there is no written menu and the waiter will reel off the list of the day's specials. They normally open for lunch and in the evening. *Ristoranti* are not always open for lunch. The food and surroundings are usually more refined than those of a trattoria. Both, however, add a cover charge, which includes bread, and a service charge to the bill.
Pizzerie specialize in pizzas, but often serve simple pasta dishes as well. Look out for *forno al legno*—pizzas cooked in a wood-fired oven.
Osterie can either be old-fashioned places specializing in home-cooked food or extremely elegant, long-established resaurants.

PAYING THE BILL

Pay by requesting the bill (*il conto*), and check to see whether service is included. Scribbled bills on scraps of paper are illegal; if you don't get a proper one, say that you need a receipt (*una recevuta*), which all restaurants, bars and shops are legally obliged to issue. Both they and you can be fined if you do not take this with you. Some smaller establishments expect to be paid in cash; you'll be able to use a credit card in more expensive establishments. If service is included, it's customary to leave a small tip—some loose change will do.

Italian cuisine Florentine-style. It's morning coffee, ice cream, wine and pasta that will stay in the memory.

Restaurants by Cuisine

There are restaurants to suit all tastes and budgets in Florence. On this page they are listed by cuisine. For a more detailed description of each restaurant, see Florence by Area.

COFFEE/PASTRIES

Caffé Amerini (▷ 47)
Caffé Pitti (▷ 91)
Cammillo (▷ 91)
Colle Bereto (▷ 48)
Gilli (▷ 48)
Guibbe Rosse (▷ 48)
Paszkowski (▷ 49)
Pillori d'Arno (▷ 50)
Rivoire (▷ 50)
Robiglio (▷ 76)

ELEGANT

Belcore (▷ 75)
Cantinetta Antinori (▷ 75)
Il Cestello (▷ 48)
Enoteca Pinchiorri (▷ 48)
Grand Hotel Incanto (▷ 49)
Hosteria Bibendum (▷ 49)
Ristorante San Michele (▷ 105)
Relais le Jardin (▷ 75)
Sabatini (▷ 76)

ICE CREAM

Festival del Gelato (▷ 48)
Gelateria Carabé (▷ 75)
Perché No! (▷ 49)
Perseo (▷ 50)
Vivoli (▷ 50)

PIZZAS/SNACKS

Baldovino (▷ 47)
La Bussolo (▷ 47)
Cantinetta dei Verrazzano (▷ 47)
Capocaccia (▷ 48)
Coquinarius (▷ 75)
O!O (▷ 92)
Procacci (▷ 50)
Munaciello (▷ 92)
Le Volpi e l'Uva (▷ 92)

TUSCAN/FLORENTINE

Alle Murate (▷ 47)
Barsotti da Guido (▷ 105)
Da Benvenuto (▷ 47)
Il Biondo (▷ 106)
Boccadama (▷ 47)
De Bruno (▷ 106)
La Buca (▷ 106)
Buca di San Antonio (▷ 105)
Il Campo (▷ 106)
Il Carmine (▷ 92)
La Casalinga (▷ 92)
Il Cibreo (▷ 48)
Coco Lezzone (▷ 48)
Gozzi Sergio (▷ 75)
Dante (▷ 105)
Il Latini (▷ 49)
Al Mangia (▷ 106)
Le Mossacce (▷ 75)
Oliviero (▷ 49)
Osteria del Cinghiale Bianco (▷ 92)
Osteria de' Benci (▷ 49)

Osteria de Logge (▷ 106)
Pallottino (▷ 49)
Palle d'Ore (▷ 75)
Ristorante I Polpa (▷ 105)
Ristorante Perseus (▷ 105)
Sotto le Fonti (▷ 106)
Taverna del Bronzino (▷ 76)
La Taverna di San Guiseppe (▷ 106)
Trattoria Ponte Vecchio (▷ 50)
Zá-Zá (▷ 76)

VEGETARIAN/ETHNIC

Belle Donne (▷ 47)
Eito (▷ 48)
Il Mandarino (▷ 49)
Osteria Santo Spirito (▷ 92)
Rose's (▷ 50)
Ruth's (▷ 76)
Trattoria Antellesi (▷ 76)
Trattoria Antichi Cancelli (▷ 76)
Trattoria da Leo (▷ 105)
Trattoria Marione (▷ 50)
Al Tranvai (▷ 92)
Il Vegetariano (▷ 76)

If You Like...

However you'd like to spend your time in Florence, these top suggestions should help you tailor your ideal visit. Each sight or listing has a fuller write-up in Florence by Area.

EXCLUSIVE SHOPPING

Descend on Via de' Tornabuoni (▷ 36) for the best in designer names—Armani, Gucci, Prada.
Sparkling gold and exquisite jewellery line either side of the Ponte Vecchio (▷ 34–35).
Florence is famed for its superb Italian shoes, and one of the best is Salvatore Ferragamo (▷ 44); you can visit the museum too (▷ 38).

TAKING A SOUVENIR HOME

Stationery—Pineider (▷ 43) has the most gorgeous array of handmade paper and bound notebooks, plus pens and desk accessories.
Ceramics—choose an authetic jug or pot from the friendly Diss (▷ 89).
Wine—all price ranges for the local Tuscan Chianti from I Sapori Del Chianti (▷ 72).

If you want to capture the true essence of Florence try all things local and take something home

EATING LOCAL CUISINE

Sit at a shared table, trying out local dishes, at Belle Donne (▷ 47).
The cuisine is Tuscan, the restaurant fashionable—try Coco Lezzone (▷ 48) for that classic meal.
Close to the bridge of the same name, try Trattoria Ponte Vecchio (▷ 50).

HISTORIC CAFÉS

Gilli (▷ 48)—watch the world go by in the Piazza della Repubblica.
Paszkowski (▷ 49)—more indulgence on the Piazza Reppublica—try the fruit tarts.
Rivoire (▷ 50)—set in the attractive Piazza Signoria, it's perfect to unwind in.

Italian ice cream at its best uses local produce and the freshest of ingredients

INDULGING IN ICE CREAM

Perché No! (▷ 49) is well-placed to relax in the Piazza Signoria for a treat.
Try a fresh fruit variety at Perseo (▷ 50)—strawberry, mango and more.
The most famous of all gelateria in Florence, Vivoli (▷ 50) changes its specials to suit the seasons.

A ROOM WITH A VIEW

Try the Hermitage (▷ 112) with its roof garden overlooking the River Arno.
For a panoramic bird's-eye view of the rooftops of Florence, try the bohemian Sorelle Bandini (▷ 109).
Some of the best views of the Tuscan countryside are from the hilltop town of Fiesole (▷ 98); for luxury as well try Villa San Michele (▷ 112).

SPLASHING OUT

Stay in the Helvetia & Bristol (▷ 112) for sheer luxury and elegance.
Shop in Via de' Tornabuoni (▷ 36) and stock your wardrobe with the top names in design.
Treat yourself to a refined cup of coffee at the stylish Paszkowski (▷ 49).

Exquisite marbled paper and beautifully presented stationery has been made for centuries

PUTTING A SMILE ON THE KIDS' FACES

The Museo Stibbert (▷ 96) has a fine collection of armour for your budding knights.
Go to the soccer stadium (▷ 104) to cheer on local team Fiorentina when they're at home.
If you need to cool off, visit the Piscina le Pavoniere (▷ 104) outdoor pool.

Buy it or just look—Italian fashion from top designer houses

FLORENCE ON A BUDGET

For good value combined with historic surroundings stay at the hotel Chiazzi (▷ 109).
If the real thing is a bit pricey, there are some great look-a-like bargains at San Lorenzo market (▷ 68).
There's no charge to see the stunning paintings in the church of Santa Felicità (▷ 87).

More delights of the city; ring the bell for a legendary cocktail

THE CITY BY NIGHT

Sip a cocktail in the world-famous nightspot, Harry's Bar (▷ 46)
Take a trip up to Piazza Michelangelo (▷ 87) to view the city in all its glory at night.
Attend a concert or opera at Florence's largest concert hall, Theatro Comunale. (▷ 74)

A LAZY MORNING

Relax over breakfast on the roof garden of a hotel such as the Hermitage (▷ 112).
Amble down to the Boboli Gardens (▷ 82), a cool oasis on a hot summer's day and just the spot for a picnic.
Take refuge in the calm and tranquillity of Santa Maria Maddelena dei Pazzi (▷ 69).

TO DO SOMETHING DIFFERENT

Try your luck on the horses at the Ippodromo delle Mulina (▷ 104). Chariot racing takes place here as well.
Hop on a bus and venture out to see some of Florence's interesting suburbs or lovely hill towns such as Fiesole (▷ 98).
Be uplifted at a recital in one of Florence's splendid churches such as Santa Maria dei Ricci (▷ 46).

There are plenty of green spaces in the city where you can relax

It doesn't take long to find a view in Florence, particularly from the top of a church such as San Miniato al Monte (right)

Florence by Area

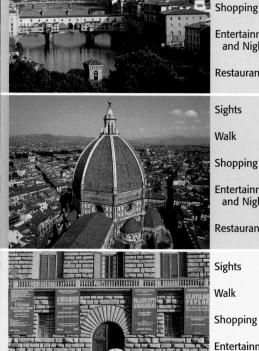

The South Centro

This district is the very heart of historic Florence. Its pedestrianized, cobbled streets and wide piazzas are a joy. Here, too, are fine Renaissance palaces and the ancient grid of medieval lanes.

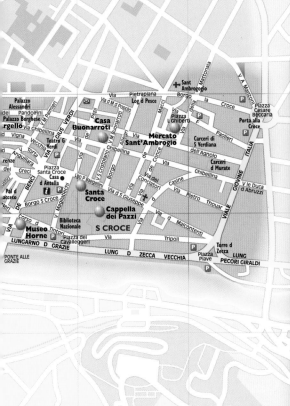

Palazzo
Alessandri
del   Pandolfini
Palazzo Borghese
rgello Via Ghibellina
d Vigna
Vecchia
renze Torre Via
del   Anguillara
Greci

**Casa
Buonarroti**

Teatro G
Verdi

Piazza
Santa Croce

**Mercato
Sant'Ambrogio**

Via
Pepi

Via d M d Popolo

Pietrapiana
Log d Pesce

✠ Sant
Ambrogio

Borgo   la   Croce

Via
Piazza
L Ghiberti

**Porta alla
Croce**

Piazza
Cesare
Beccaria

Carceri di
S Verdiana

Carceri di
S Verdiana

V A Mattonala

V.A Mattonala

Mattonala

Marci

**Carceri
d Murate**

dell'Agnolo

Ghibellina

V le Duca
d Abruzzi

Via del
Conidori

Casine

Via   Pietro   Thouar

ITALIA

Via del
Malcontenti

Pál d
acceso

Casa
d Antella

**Santa
Croce**

**Cappella
dei Pazzi**

Biblioteca
Nazionale

Piazza dei
Cavalleggeri

**Museo
Horne**

Corso d

Borgo S Croce

DE

Verri

BENCI

LUNGARNO D GRAZIE

PONTE ALLE
GRAZIE

S CROCE

Via

Tripoli

LUNG   D   ZECCA   VECCHIA

Torre d
Zecca

Piazza
Piave

LUNG
PECORI GIRALDI

GIOVINE

VIALE

G   H   J

The South Centro

Bargello

- Donatello's *David*
- Giambologna's *Mercury*
- Giambologna's animals
- Michelangelo's *Bacchus*
- Della Robbia's terracottas
- Courtyard

TIP

- The museum is very popular and in high season it is best to book in advance.

The Bargello, with its airy courtyard, is so pleasant that you would want to visit it even if it were not home to what is arguably the finest collection of Renaissance sculpture in the world.

Diverse uses Built in 1255, the Bargello was the first seat of Florence's city government and served as the city's main law court before being passed to the *Bargello* (Chief of Police) in 1574; it was used as a prison until 1859. In 1865 it opened as a museum, with an unrivalled collection of Renaissance sculpture and decorative arts.

Courtyard art The courtyard walls, once the site of executions, carry the coats of arms of the *Podestà* (chief magistrates), whose headquarters were here, and 16th-century sculpture, including

The Bargello viewed from the Campanile (far left). Inside the vaulted Bargello (left). The plaque of Christina de'Medici (right). Courtyard of the Bargello (below left). Stained glass crest (below middle left). The striking façade of the Bargello (below middle right). Bust of Piero di Lorenzo di Medici (below right)

Giambologna's *Oceanus* from the Boboli Gardens (▷ 82). The ground floor has works by Michelangelo, Cellini and Giambologna, including *Mercury* (1564).

Sculpture, medals and bronzes In the Salone del Consiglio Generale, a vaulted hall on the first floor that was once the courtroom, works by Donatello include his decidedly camp bronze *David* (*c*1430–40), dressed in long boots and a jaunty hat (the first freestanding nude since the Roman period), and his *St. George* (1416), sculpted for the exterior of Orsanmichele (▷ 39). On the second floor enamelled terracottas by the della Robbia family include the bust of a boy by Andrea della Robbia. Note the displays of Italian medals and small Renaissance bronzes. The arms room has ivory-inlay saddles, guns and armour.

THE BASICS

✚ G6
✉ Via del Proconsolo 4
☎ 055 238 8606
🕐 Daily 8.15–1.50 (last admission 40 mins before closing); closed 1st, 3rd, 5th Sun, 2nd, 4th Mon of month and 1 Jan, 1 May, 25 Dec
🚌 14, 23, A
🚹 Good
💲 Moderate

THE SOUTH CENTRO

★ TOP 25

25

Cappella dei Pazzi

Monochrome interior of the Cappella dei Pazzi (left). The serene cloisters and chapel (right)

THE BASICS

🔷 H6
✉ Piazza Santa Croce
☎ 055 244 619
🕐 Apr–end Oct Mon–Sat 9.30– 5.30, Sun 1–5; Nov–end Mar Mon–Sat 8–12.30, 3–5.30, Sun 1–5.30
🚌 14, 23, C
♿ Good
💷 Moderate

HIGHLIGHTS

● Cappella dei Pazzi
● Cloister
● Roundels of the evangelists
● Cimabue's crucifix (13th century)
● Taddeo Gaddi's fresco (1333)
● Donatello's *St. Louis of Toulouse* (1424)

In contrast to the adjacent church of Santa Croce, a key stop on the tourist circuit, the cloisters are not much visited. The solitude is perfect for appreciating their grace and harmony.

Convent building On the south side of Santa Croce are the buildings of a former convent. These include the Cappella dei Pazzi, one of the great architectural masterpieces of the early Renaissance, and a 14th-century refectory, which houses the Museo dell'Opera di Santa Croce. This is one of the lowest areas in Florence, and to the left of the Cappella dei Pazzi a plaque almost 6m (20ft) up shows the high point of the November 1966 floodwaters. The second cloister, a haven of calm, was designed by Filippo Brunelleschi.

The Pazzi Chapel The Cappella, which was commissioned as a chapter house by Andrea dei Pazzi and designed by Brunelleschi (*c*1430), is incorporated into the cloisters. This domed chapel is done in grey *pietra serena* (grey sandstone) against a white plaster background, embellished only by enamelled terracotta roundels.

Small but beautiful The museum contains many important works, including a restored crucifix by Giovanni Cimabue. On the walls a huge fresco by Taddeo Gaddi shows the Last Supper, the Tree of Life, St. Louis of Toulouse, St. Francis, St. Benedict and Mary Magdalene washing Christ's feet. Prominent is the gilded bronze statue of *St. Louis of Toulouse* (1424), sculpted by Donatello.

This way to the science musem (left). The astrolabe of the Gualtiero Arsenio (right)

Museo di Storia della Scienza

Here you'll find a fascinating collection of scientific instruments, a reminder that the Florentine Renaissance was not only an artistic movement, but also fostered the origins of modern science.

Pure science In the 14th-century Palazzo Castellani, the Museum of the History of Science housed a well-organized collection, which in large part belonged to the Medici Grand Dukes. In 1775 the Museum of Physics and Natural Sciences was opened and in 1929 the collection was moved to its current location. The galleries are on the first and second floors; the ground floor is the library of the Istituto di Storia della Scienza.

Galileo Galilei There is a sizeable exhibition devoted to Galileo (1564–1642), Pisa-born but adopted by the Medici as the court mathematician. Some exhibits border on the hagiographic: His telescope is there, but also the middle finger of his right hand, preserved in a reliquary.

More exhibits The map room has a 16th-century map of the world by the Portuguese cartographer Lopo Homem, revealing the limit of European geographical knowledge at that time: Australasia is nowhere to be found and the tip of South America fades into blankness. It also has a collection of armillary spheres, used to divine the movements of the planets. On the second floor is a series of 18th-century wax and ceramic models of birth deformities, complete with helpful hints for the doctor, such as where to insert the forceps.

THE BASICS

www.imss.fi.it

🕂 F6

✉ Piazza dei Guidici 1

☎ 055 265 311

🕐 Oct–end May Mon, Wed–Sat 9.30–5, Tue 9.30–1, (2nd Sun each month 10–1); Jun–end Sep Mon, Wed, Thu, Fri 9.30–5, Tue, Sat 9.30–1 (last admission 30 mins before closing)

🚍 23, B

♿ Excellent

💲 Expensive

❓ Excellent guide book

HIGHLIGHTS

● Galileo's telescope
● Lopo Homem's map of the world (16th century)
● Antonio Santucci's armillary sphere (1573)
● Copy of Lorenzo della Volpaia's clock of the planets (1593)

Piazza della Signoria

TOP 25

The Piazza Signoria is a gathering place—from protests to costumed parades

THE BASICS

- F6
- Piazza della Signoria
- 23, A, B
- Good

HIGHLIGHTS

- Loggia dei Lanzi (1376)
- Cellini's *Perseus* (1554)
- Giambologna's *Rape of the Sabine Women* (1583)
- Ammannati's *Neptune* (1575)
- Rivoire café
- Sorbi newspaper and post-card kiosk

Standing in the Piazza della Signoria in the shadow of the grim, forbidding Palazzo Vecchio, it is impossible to escape the sense of Florence's past political might.

Political piazza The Piazza della Signoria has been the hub of political life in Florence since the 14th century. It was the scene of great triumphs, such as the return of the Medici in 1530, but also of the Bonfire of the Vanities instigated by Savonarola, who was himself burned at the stake here in 1498, denounced as a heretic by the Inquisition.

Significant sculptures The sculptures here bristle with political connotations, many of them fiercely contradictory. Michelangelo's *David* (the original is in the Accademia) was placed outside the Palazzo Vecchio as a symbol of the Republic's defiance of the tyrannical Medici. The *Neptune* (1575), by Ammannati, celebrates the Medici's maritime ambitions, and Giambologna's statue of *Duke Cosimo I* (1595) the man who brought all of Tuscany under Medici military rule. The statue of Perseus holding Medusa's head, by Cellini (1554), is a stark reminder of what happened to those who crossed the Medici. The graceful Loggia dei Lanzi, which functions as an open-air sculpture gallery, was designed by Orcagna in 1376.

Postcard paradise Sorbi, the newspaper kiosk, has an unrivalled collection of postcards and newspapers, which you could enjoy over a drink in the Rivoire café (▷ 50).

Aerial view of Santa Croce (left). Detail of frescoes by Giotto in Santa Croce (right)

Santa Croce

Despite its vast size and swarms of tourists, Santa Croce is personal and touchingly intimate, perhaps because of the sense that one somehow knows the people buried here.

Burial place Santa Croce, rebuilt for the Franciscan order in 1294 by Arnolfo di Cambio, is the burial place of the great and the good in Florence. Michelangelo is buried in Santa Croce, as are Rossini, Machiavelli and the Pisa-born Galileo Galilei, who was excommunicated during the Inquisition and was not allowed a Christian burial until 1737, 95 years after his death. There is also a memorial to Dante, whose sarcophagus is empty.

Anglophile The church exterior is covered with a polychrome marble façade added in 1863 and paid for by the English benefactor Sir Francis Sloane. It looks over the Piazza Santa Croce, site of an annual football game in medieval costume.

Artistic riches The artistic wealth in Santa Croce is stunning; frescos by Gaddi (1380) in the Cappella Maggiore tell the story of the holy cross ('Santa Croce') and beautiful frescos by Giotto in the Bardi and Peruzzi chapels show scenes from the lives of St. Francis and St. John the Evangelist. Don't miss the memorial to 19th-century playwright Giovanni Battista Nicolini, left of the entrance facing the altar, said to have inspired the *Statue of Liberty*. Santa Croce was severely hit by flooding in 1966, and you can still see a tide mark showing far up on the pillars and walls.

THE BASICS

⊞ H6
✉ Piazza Santa Croce
☎ 055 244 619; museum 055 246 105
🕐 Apr–end Oct Mon–Sat 9.30–5.30, Sun 1–5; Nov–end Mar Mon–Sat 8–12.30, 3–5.30, Sun 1–5.30; closed during services
🚌 14, 23, C
♿ Good
💶 Moderate with museum

HIGHLIGHTS

● Giotto's frescoes (1320–25)
● Tombs of Michelangelo, Machiavelli, Galileo
● Painted wooden ceiling
● Donatello's *Annunciation* (1435)
● Polychrome marble façade (1863)

Galleria degli Uffizi

TOP 25

HIGHLIGHTS

● The Tribune (room 18)
● Giotto's *Ognissanti Madonna* (1310)
● Botticelli's *Birth of Venus* (1485) and *Primavera* (c1480)
● Piero della Francesca's *Federico da Montefeltro and Battista Sforza* (1460)
● Leonardo's *Annunciation* (1472–75) and *Adoration of the Magi* (1481)
● Michelangelo's *Holy Family* (1508)
● Titian's *Venus of Urbino* (1538)

TIPS

● Reserve in advance; waiting can be up to 3 hours.
● Plan what you want to see as backtracking is difficult.
● Be patient, highlights are often blocked by large groups.
● There are frequent long waits for the toilet, go before you arrive.

The Uffizi encompasses the artistic developments of the Renaissance and beyond. It is a powerful expression of Florence's extraordinary role in the history of art.

Medici art The gallery contains part of the Medici's art collection, bequeathed in 1737 by Anna Maria Luisa. The building was designed by Vasari, in the 1560s, as the administrative offices (*uffizi*) of the Grand Duchy. Parts of the building and collection that were damaged by the 1993 bomb were restored and reopened in 1998.

From sculpture to painting Today people come for the paintings, but until the 19th century the attraction was sculpture (mostly now in the Bargello, ▷ 24). The collection is displayed in chronological order, starting with the first stirrings

Serene detail of the Madonna in the Uffizi (far left). Crowds gather outside the Uffizi (middle). The Holy Family by Michelangelo (right). Artisitic magnificence in the gallery (below left). On the Ponte Vecchio bridge linking to the Uffizi gallery (below middle). The gallery seen from the River Arno (below right)

of the Renaissance in the 13th century and ending with works by Caravaggio, Rembrandt and Canaletto from the 17th and 18th centuries. Uccello's *Battle of San Romano* (1456) exemplifies the technical advances of the Renaissance, while Filippo Lippi's *Madonna and Child with Two Angels* (c1465) reveals the emotional focus typical of the period.

Venus Perhaps most fascinating is the Tribune, an octagonal chamber with a mother-of-pearl ceiling. In the middle is the Medici *Venus*, whose sensuous derrière earned her the reputation of the sexiest sculpture of the ancient world. Portraits include Bronzino's *Giovanni de Medici* (c1549), a smiling boy holding a goldfinch. The café provides a welcome pit-stop and has superb views of Piazza della Signoria.

THE BASICS

www.uffizi.firenze.it
✚ F6
✉ Loggiato degli Uffizi 6
☎ 055 238 8651.
(Reserve ahead to avoid lines by calling 055 294 833)
🕐 Tue–Sun 8.15–6.50 (last admission 45 mins before closing); closed 1 May
🚌 23, B
♿ Good
💶 Expensive

Palazzo Vecchio

The striking Palazzo Vecchio dominating the skyline has many intricate details within

THE BASICS

- ✚ F6
- ✉ Piazza della Signoria
- ☎ 055 276 8465
- 🕐 Mon–Wed, Fri, Sun 9–7, Thu 9–2 (also late opening Mon, Fri in summer)
- 🚌 23, A, B
- ♿ Good
- 💶 Expensive
- ❓ In summer, walks along the parapets and other parts of the Palazzo Vecchio not usually open to the public are arranged. Details from the tourist information office

HIGHLIGHTS

- Sala delle Carte
- Sala dei Gigli
- Michelangelo's *Victory*
- Donatello's *Judith and Holofernes*
- View from the Terrazza di Saturno
- Salone dei Cinquecento

With its fortresslike castellations and its commanding 95m (311ft) bell tower, the Palazzo Vecchio conveys a message of political power supported by solid military strength.

Town Hall The Palazzo Vecchio is still Florence's town hall, as it has been since its completion by Arnolfo di Cambio in 1302. It was substantially remodelled for Duke Cosimo I, who made it his palace in 1540. It became known as the Palazzo Vecchio (Old Palace) when Cosimo transferred his court to the Palazzo Pitti. During the brief period when Florence was the capital of Italy (1865–71), it housed the Parliament and Foreign Ministry.

Assembly room The vast Salone dei Cinquecento is 53.5m by 22m (175ft by 72ft); 18m (59ft) high and was designed in the 1490s, during the era of the Florentine Republic, as the meeting place of the 500-strong ruling assembly. Vasari painted the military scenes of Florence's victory over Siena and Pisa (1563–65). The theme of Florence's might is underscored by Michelangelo's *Victory* (1533–34), as well as sculptures of the *Labours of Hercules* by Vincenzo dei Rossi.

Loggia views On the second floor the Terrazza di Saturno is an open loggia with views to the hills. The Sala dei Gigli is decorated with gold fleurs-de-lys and houses Donatello's *Judith and Holofernes* (1456–60). The Sala delle Carte (Map Room), has a wonderful collection of globes and maps painted on leather, showing the world in 1563.

Ponte Vecchio

HIGHLIGHTS

● Gold and jewellery shops
● Views of the Arno
● Corridoio Vasariano (1565)
● Bust of Cellini (1900)

No visit to Florence is complete without a saunter down this bridge; lined with old shops jutting precariously over the water, it is difficult to believe you're on a proper bridge and not just strolling down a narrow street.

TIP

● The sun sets directly downriver from the bridge, and the golden tones of the structure itself are magical on a good evening.

The test of time Near the Roman crossing, the Old Bridge was, until 1218, the only bridge across the Arno in Florence. The current bridge was rebuilt after a flood in 1345. During World War II, it was the only bridge the Germans did not destroy but they blocked access by demolishing the medieval buildings either side. On 4 November 1966 the bridge survived when the Arno burst its banks.

Private path When the Medici moved from the Palazzo Vecchio to the Palazzo Pitti, they decided

The vaulted arcades of the Ponte Vecchio were rebuilt in 1453 by Michelozzo (left). Bust of sculptor, soldier and goldsmith Benvenuto Cellini guarding the bridge (below left). The Ponte Veccchio at dusk (below middle). Detail of a section of the bridge (below right). Gold has been sold on the Ponte Vecchio for centuries (below)

they needed a connecting route from the Uffizi to the Palazzo Pitti on the other side of the river that enabled them to keep out of contact—heaven forbid!—with their people. The result was Vasari's *Corridoio Vasariano*, built in 1565 on top of the buildings lining the bridge's eastern parapet.

Glitz Shops have been on the Ponte Vecchio since the 13th century: initially all types—butchers and fishmongers and later tanners, whose industrial waste caused a pretty rank stench. In 1593, Medici Duke Ferdinand I decreed that only goldsmiths and jewellers be allowed on the bridge. When the shops close their wooden shutters it makes them look like suitcases. As one of the places that Florentines regularly come to for the *passeggiata*, it is also always full of Senegalese street vendors, hawking fake goods.

THE BASICS

✚ F6
🚌 B, D
♿ Good

Via de' Tornabuoni

History meets style on the smartest street in town

THE BASICS

🔲 E5–E6
✉ Via de' Tornabuoni
🚌 23, A, B
♿ Good

HIGHLIGHTS

● Sassetti Chapel frescoes in Santa Trinità
● Ferragamo Shoe Museum
● Designer shops
● Palazzo Strozzi
● 17th-century façade of San Gaetano

Florence maybe one of the world's richest cultural cities, but it's also a place for serious shopping. Fashionable Via de' Tornabuoni supports the top names in fashion, set among the stunning palaces.

Shopping in palaces Italy has always been synonymous with style, think Milan or Rome, but Florence contributes in its own way, too. The city hosted Italy's earliest fashion shows in the 1950s, and innovative designers made their fortunes within the city's medieval palaces here on Via de' Tornabuoni. Salvatore Ferragamo, the flagship store and shoe museum (▷ 38), can be found within the Palazzo Spini-Feroni, one of the best preserved private medieval palaces in Florence; while Guccio Gucci picked this street—three generations ago—for his headquarters, which is still based at 73r Tornabuoni. You may be intent on a bargain but spare a moment to glance up at the façades and interiors of the imposing buildings.

Beyond the shops At the north end of the street is the stunning Palazzo Antinori (1465), next to the city's greatest baroque church San Gaetano (1648), a tranquil spot to escape the crowds. Halfway down is the impressive Palazzo Strozzi. At the end is Piazza Santa Trinità with its artistically rich church. Central to the square is the tall Column of Justice, brought from the Baths of Caracalla in Rome and given to Cosimo I in 1560 by Pope Pius IV. Just beyond here is the Santa Trinità Bridge (▷ 39) that links elegant Tornabuoni with Oltrano on the south bank of the River Arno.

More to See

BADIA FIORENTINA

The Badia Fiorentina, the oldest monastery in Florence, was founded in AD978 by Willa, widow of Umberto, Margrave of Tuscany. It is best known in connection with Dante, who used to meet Beatrice here. It's has a magnificent bell tower, which is Gothic at the top and Romanesque at the base. Inside are two fine works of art, namely Filippino Lippi's *The Madonna Appearing to St. Bernard*, to the left of the entrance, and the tomb of Count Ugo, son of Willa and Umberto.

➕ G6 ✉ Piazza San Firenze, entrance in Via Dante Alighieri ☎ 055 287 389 🕐 Mon 3–6 🚌 14, 23, A ♿ Impossible 💷 Free

CASA BUONARROTI

www.casabuonaroti.it

This house, which Michelangelo bought in 1508, is now a fascinating museum and gallery. Exhibits include the artist's earliest known work, the *Madonna della Scala* (*c*1491), a wood and wax model (the only one of its type) of a river god and a model of the façade for San Lorenzo never executed.

➕ H6 ✉ Via Ghibellina 70 ☎ 055 241 752 🚌 A, 14 🕐 Wed–Mon 9.30–2 ♿ Poor 💷 Expensive

CASA DI DANTE

The 13th-century House of Dante has been restored and contains material relating to author's life and work.

➕ F6 ✉ Via Santa Margherita 1 ☎ 055 219 416 🕐 Tue–Sat 10–5, Sun 10–1, 1st Sun of each month 10–4; closed last Sun of each month 🚌 A ♿ None 💷 Moderate

MERCATO NUOVO

So called to distinguish it from the Mercato Vecchio, which used to be on the site of what is now the Piazza della Repubblica, this market is most famous for the engaging brass boar with a shiny, well-stroked nose, *Il Porcellino*, which sometimes lends its name to the market. It is also known as the 'straw market', a reference to the straw hats historically sold here.

➕ F6 ✉ Piazza Mercato Nuovo 🕐 Apr–end Oct daily 9–8; Nov–end Mar Tue–Sun 9–6; closed Sun, Mon in winter 🍴 Yes 🚌 6, 11, 36, 37, A ♿ Good (but crowded)

The ceiling of the Badia Fiorentina is decorated with beautiful 15th-century frescoes (above)

A popular pig in the Mercato Nuovo (left)

MERCATO DI SANT'AMBROGIO

After the Mercato Centrale, this is the second most important market for fresh produce in Florence. It attracts Florence's working population, is inexpensive and is pleasantly noisy.

✚ H6　✉ Piazza Lorenzo Ghiberti
🕐 Mon–Sat 7–2　🍴 Yes　🚌 A　♿ Good

MUSEO HORNE

This delightful small museum, housed in Palazzo Corsi, owes its existence to the English art historian and collector Herbert Percy Horne (1864–1916). Horne bought the palazzo in 1904 for his interesting collection of paintings, furniture and sculpture. On his death, he left the palazzo and its contents to the Italy.

✚ G7　✉ Via de Benci 6　☎ 055 244 661
🕐 Mon–Sat 9–1; closed hols　🚌 23, B, C
♿ None　🎟 Moderate

MUSEO SALVATORE FERRAGAMO

Founded in 1995, this collection of 10,000 pairs of shoes by Ferragamo dates from his return from Hollywood to Florence in 1927 until his death in the 1960s. The collection highlights Ferragamo's choice of hues, his imaginative models and experimentation with materials. Many examples were created for celebrities, such as Marilyn Monroe and Greta Garbo.

✚ E6　✉ Palazzo Spini Feroni, Via de' Tornabuoni 2　☎ 055 336 0456　🕐 Mon–Fri 9–1, 2–6　🚌 A, B　♿ Poor　🎟 Free

OGNISSANTI

This was the parish church of the Vespucci family, and it was also the church of Botticelli's family; he was buried here. In the second chapel on the right facing the altar is a fresco by Ghirlandaio, which is said to include Amerigo's portrait (the boy standing behind the Virgin). In the *cenacolo* (refectory) there are more Ghirlandaio pieces—a *Last Supper* and *St. Jerome in his Study*—and Botticelli's *St. Augustine in his Study*.

✚ D5　✉ Borgo Ognissanti 42　☎ 055 239 8700　🕐 Daily 7–12.30, 4–8. Convent Mon, Tue, Sat 8–12, 4.45–6.30　🚌 12, B　♿ Fair
🎟 Free

An emblem on the Church of the Ognissanti (left)
Magnificent 17th- and 18th-century frescoes adorn the ceiling and walls of the Ognissanti (right)

ORSANMICHELE

Built as a grain market in 1337, Orsanmichele became a church in 1380. The city's guilds commissioned some of the best artists to make statues of patron saints to sit in the canopied niches, and so created a permanent outdoor exhibition of 15th-century Florentine sculpture. These statues are being removed one by one for restoration and copies put in their place. Some of the original works are still there, including Lorenzo Ghiberti's bronzes of St. Matthew (1419–22).

➕ F6 ⊠ Via dei Calzaiuoli ☎ 055 284 944 🕐 Tue–Sun 10–5 ♿ Good ▮ Free

PIAZZA DELLA REPUBBLICA

This grandiose square in the middle of Florence, on the site of the old market, was built in the 1870s, when Florence briefly was the capital of Italy. Florentines are not fond of the square's architecture nor its crass neo-classical triumphal arch, but it is an unusually large open space, where you can breathe a little and let a child

run free. All around are excellent grand cafés, if somewhat overpriced.

➕ F5 ⊠ A ♿ Good

PONTE SANTA TRINITÀ

The finest of Florence's bridges dates back to 1252, although what you see today is a well-executed replica of Ammannati's bridge built in 1567 and destroyed by the Nazis in 1944. Ammannati was commissioned by Cosimo I and probably consulted Michelangelo in his designs. Some of the loveliest views of Florence, especially the Ponte Vecchio, are to be had from here.

➕ E6 ⊠ Ponte Santa Trinità 🚌 6, 11, 36, 37, B, D ♿ Good ▮ Free

SAN MARTINO DEL VESCOVO

This tiny oratory is situated right in the heart of medieval Florence and is a rewarding stop on a day of doing the big sites. Don't miss the lunette frescos on the upper walls.

➕ F6 ⊠ Piazza San Martino, Via Dante Alighieri 🕐 Mon–Sat 10–12, 3–5 🚌 A ♿ Acceptable ▮ Free

The city's guild workers depicted on the wall of the Orsanmichele

Summer, *one of the 'Seasons' statues on the Ponte San Trinità*

Dante's Florence

A short walk through the district where Dante lived, worked and played and on then to the eastern part of the city to Sante Croce.

DISTANCE: 1km (0.5 miles) approx **ALLOW:** 1 hour including visits

START

BATTISTERO (▷ 55)
✚ F5 🚌 1, 14, 23, A

END

SANTA CROCE (▷ 29)
✚ H6 🚌 14, 23, C

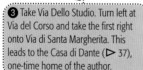

① Start at the Baptistery (▷ 55), where the poet Dante Alighieri was baptized. At that time, it was not covered with the marble facing that adorns the façade today.

② According to tradition Dante watched the construction of the cathedral from the Sasso di Dante, a stone (marked) in the wall between Via dello Studio and Via del Proconsolo, opposite the Duomo.

③ Take Via Dello Studio. Turn left at Via del Corso and take the first right onto Via di Santa Margherita. This leads to the Casa di Dante (▷ 37), one-time home of the author.

④ Opposite is San Martino del Vescovo (▷ 39), where Dante's family worshipped. Back towards Via del Corso is Santa Margherita, where his Beatrice went to Mass.

⑧ Dante's sarcophagus, inside the church, is empty. Despite all his connections with the city of Florence, Dante was buried in Ravenna.

⑦ Take Via dell'Anguillara until you come to Piazza Santa Croce. The streets around here are dotted with artisans' workshops. Outside the church of Santa Croce (▷ 29) there is a 19th-century statue of Dante.

⑥ Dante often saw Beatrice here and the Badia's bell would have punctuated Dante's daily life. Exit and turn onto Via del Proconsolo, past the Bargello (▷ 24–25), which was being built in Dante's time.

⑤ From Santa Margherita turn left onto Via Dante Alighieri for the entrance of the Badia (▷ 37).

WALK

THE SOUTH CENTRO

Shopping

ANGELA CAPUTI

Angela Caputi is the place to look for bright, bold and highly original costume jewellery. Clothing and accessories to go with the pendant or earrings you have just bought are also stocked.

🚩 F6 ✉ Borgo Santi Apostoli 44–46r ☎ 055 292 993 🚌 B

ARMANDO POGGI

One of the widest selections of porcelain in the city. Stocks Guiseppi Armani figurines and Richard Ginori porcelain.

🚩 F5 ✉ Via Calzaiuoli 103r & 116r ☎ 055 211 719 🚌 A

BACCANI

A beautiful shop, established in 1903. The old interior is filled with prints, engravings, paintings and old maps. Prices vary from very reasonable to very expensive.

🚩 E6 ✉ Via della Vigna Nuova 75r ☎ 055 214 467 🚌 6, A

IL BISONTE

With everything stamped with the trademark bison, this brand is at the cutting edge of leather bags and accessories.

🚩 E6 ✉ Via del Parione 31r ☎ 055 215 772 🚌 6, 11, 36, 37, A, B

LA BOGETTA DELLA FRUTTA

The owners search high and low for more unusual products to cram the shelves of this family-run

business. The carefully selected produce includes fresh fruit, cheese, yogurts, pasta, balsamic vinegar and wine.

🚩 E5 ✉ Via dei Federighi 31r ☎ 055 239 8590 🚌 6, A

BVLGARI

Florence's branch of the world-famous fashion jeweller and watchmaker.

🚩 E6 ✉ Via de' Tornabuoni 63r ☎ 055 396 786 🚌 6, 11, 22, 36, 37, A

CELLERINI

Elegant and sophisticated leather bags of outstanding quality. Styles tend to be wonderfully simple yet cleverly designed. Popular among *fashionistas*.

🚩 E5 ✉ Via del Sole 37 ☎ 055 282 533 🚌 36, 37, A

GOLD FACTS

A dazzling array of gold is for sale all over Florence, most notably on the Ponte Vecchio. In 1593 Ferdinand I decreed that only goldsmiths and jewellers should work there and it has remained that way ever since. The gold sold in Florence is 18 carat, often expressed as a rather confusing 750 per cent (with the per cent sign actually referring to 1000). Gold is also found–at somewhat lower prices–in the Santa Croce area, where, in accordance with tradition, all gold jewellery and other items are sold by weight.

CITTÀ DI SAN GALLO

This lace and linen firm was founded in 1922, and is still owned by the same family. Surviving destruction caused by the war and the 1966 floods, the tiny shop still touts it wares in a period-style atmosphere.

🚩 F6 ✉ Via Por Santa Maria 60r ☎ 055 239 6249 🚌 B

COIN

A huge clothing and design emporium with a vast range of goods at reasonable prices on the Via dei Calzaiuoli. Open on Sunday.

🚩 F5 ✉ Via dei Calzaiuoli 56r ☎ 055 280 531 🚌 A

COSE DEL PASSATO

An antiques shop specializing in vintage ceramics from Montelupo, where pottery was originally made for the Medici court.

🚩 E5 ✉ Via dei Fossi 3–5r ☎ 055 294 689 🚌 36, 37, A

DUCCI

There is a massive selection of tinted lithographs and prints here, both framed and unframed. Some unusual objects d'art are also sold, including wood carvings.

🚩 E6 ✉ Lungarno Corsini 24r ☎ 055 214 550 🚌 6, 11, 36, 37, B

EMILIO CAVALLINI

A wonderfully wacky collection of socks and hosiery.

🇪6 ✉ Via della Vigna Nuova 24r ☎ 055 238 2789 🚌 6, A

EMILIO PUCCI

A renowned Florentine fashion house created in 1950 by Marquis Emilio Pucci. This store on Via de' Tornabuoni sells fantastic, very pricey separates, silk shirts, shoes and accessories. The classy couture collection is located at Palazzo de' Pucci 6.

🇪6 ✉ Via de' Tornabuoni 20–22r ☎ 055 265 8082 🚌 6, 11, 22, 36, 37, A

FRATELLI PICCINI

If you want to go jewellery shopping on the Ponte Vecchio, make sure you take in Piccini's. They have lovely gold charms that make a nice gift, either for a loved one or yourself.

🇫6 ✉ Ponte Vecchio 23 ☎ 055 294 768 🚌 B, D

FRATELLI ROSSETTI

Beautiful shoes in classic Italian styles.

🇫5 ✉ Piazza della Repubblica 43–45r ☎ 055 216 656 🚌 A

FURLA

Chic, handsomely designed leather bags and belts at prices that are less astronomic than elsewhere. There is another branch of the store in Via della Vigna Nouva.

🇫5 ✉ Via Calzaiuoli 47r ☎ 055 238 2883 🚌 A

THE GOLD CORNER

This frequent tour-group stop in Piazza Sante Croce sells gold by weight along with typical Italian cameos and coral.

🇬6 ✉ Piazza Santa Croce 15r ☎ 055 241 971; fax 055 247 8437 🚌 23, C

GUALTIERI GANDOLFI

If you are looking for antique jewellery, this little shop just off Borgo Santi Apostoli has some amazing pieces. Check out the gem stones, glass beads and jet, as well as pieces unique to this area.

🇫6 ✉ Piazza del Limbo 8r ☎ 055 283 318 🚌 B

STYLISH CITY

One of Florence's many claims to fame is as the headquarters of Gucci. It was also in Florence, in 1927, that Salvatore Ferragamo established himself, after having made his reputation in Hollywood crafting shoes for the likes of Greta Garbo, Vivien Leigh, Gloria Swanson and the gladiators in Cecil B de Mille costume epics. This family still administers a fashion empire, producing accessories and clothes as well as the trademark shoes. Ties are also for sale in Florence at remarkably good prices. The market of San Lorenzo is the least expensive place, but even on the Ponte Vecchio the prices are agreeable!

GUCCI

A predictably elegant and pricey shop; headquarters of the Gucci empire.

🇪6 ✉ Via de' Tornabuoni 73r ☎ 055 264 5432 🚌 6, 11, 22, 36, 37, A

LEATHER SCHOOL OF SANTA CROCE

At the back of the famous church, off Via di San Giuseppe, this workshop was once run by Franciscan monks and sells quality craftsmanship at the on-site shop.

🇬6 ✉ Piazza Santa Croce 16 ☎ 055 244 533 🚌 23, B, C

LUISA

A popular spot for Florence's image-conscious men and women. Eye-catching window displays conceal a sleek interior over two floors divided into avant-garde boutiques where you'll find well-known labels rubbing shoulders with Luisa's own designs.

🇫5 ✉ Via Roma 19–21r ☎ 055 217 826 🚌 A

MARTELLI

This Florence institution has manufactured handmade gloves for more than 38 years. You would be hard pushed to find such an amazing selection elsewhere in every hue and fabric imaginable, including exquisite soft leather for men and women.

🇫6 ✉ Via Por Santa Maria 18r ☎ 055 239 6395 🚌 B

MAX & CO

The trendy branch of Max Mara sells well-designed high-fashion pieces to a mainly teenage clientele, plus a range of classics with a contemporary twist.

⊞ F5 ⊠ Via dei Calzaiuoli 89r ☎ 055 288 656 🚍 A

MISURI

This is one of the best Santa Croce area leather factories.

⊞ G6 ⊠ Piazza Santa Croce 20r ☎ 055 240 995 🚍 23, C

ORE DUE

Close to the Uffizi and producing items using the same techniques as the original Florentine goldsmiths. The styles are very traditional and are set in 18-carat gold. Prices are not over the top considering the quality of the materials and the crafsmanship involved.

⊞ F6 ⊠ Via Lambertesca 12r ☎ 055 292 143 🚍 B

PAMPALONI

As well as ceramics this high-quality gift shop, aimed at the wedding-present market, has a range of silverware and porcelain.

⊞ F6 ⊠ Borgo Santi Apostoli 47r ☎ 055 289 094 🚍 B

PARENTI

Even those who say they don't like jewellery end up ooing and aahing at Parenti's eclectic mix of styles and shapes, ranging from art nouveau to sheer 1970s glitz.

⊞ E6 ⊠ Via de' Tornabuoni 93r ☎ 055 214 438 🚍 6, 11, 22, 36, 37, A

PARIONE

This prestigious chain of stationers selling hand-decorated marbled paper, personalized stationery and accessories also has a collection of beautifully crafted music boxes and miniatures.

⊞ E6 ⊠ Via Parione 10 ☎ 055 215 684 🚍 6, 11, 22, 36, 37, A

PEGNA

This lovely old-fashioned shop, around since 1860, sells its delicious foods supermarket-style. You can buy fine cheeses, olive oils, cakes, wines,

WHAT'S AN ANTIQUE

Under Italian law an antique need not be old, but need only be made of old materials. For this reason, what would be called reproduction elsewhere is called an antique in Italy. Many shops in Florence sell antiques, from the glamorous international emporia on Borgo Ognissanti to the flea market in Piazza dei Ciompi–there are whole streets of them. The most important include Borgo Ognissanti and Via Maggio, for very expensive antiques finely displayed.

salamis, chocolates and lots more.

⊞ F5 ⊠ Via dello Studio 8 ☎ 055 282 701 🚍 A

PIANEGONDA

This silversmith uses clear and twinkling amethysts, topaz and moonstones alongside bold, sometimes theatrical styles. The pieces are ultra modern but do not lack charm and the prices are reasonable.

⊞ F5 ⊠ Via dei Calzaiuoli 96r ☎ 055 214 941 🚍 A

PINEIDER

A chic and expensive stationery and bookbindings business that was founded in 1774. One of the characteristic papers covering diaries and address books is decorated with great artists' signatures.

⊞ F6 ⊠ Piazza della Signoria 13r ☎ 055 284 655 🚍 A, B

PRADA

The world's most popular Italian fashion house of the moment. The headquarters are in Milan but there's a good range of clothes, shoes, bags and accessories in this branch.

⊞ E6 ⊠ Via de' Tornabuoni 53r ☎ 055 267 471 🚍 6, 11, 22, 36, 37, A

PRINCIPE

Classic, expensive clothes for men, women and kids.

⊞ E5 ⊠ Via del Sole 2r ☎ 055 292 764 🚍 6, 11, 36, 22, 37, A

LA RINASCENTE

This classy department store is where smart Florentines shop. It drips designer labels, although prices are good and there's the odd find to be made. There are also perfumery, lingerie and other departments for those who like to shop for everything under one roof.

🔳 F5 ⊠ Piazza della Repubblica ☎ 055 219 311 🚌 A

ROBERTO CAVALLI

One of Tuscany's most renowned designers, known for his flamboyant styles using fur and wild prints, opened his doors at this exclusive address in 2004. Take time-out at Café Cavalli.

🔳 E6 ⊠ Via de' Tornabuoni 83r ☎ 055 239 6226 🚌 6, 11, 22, 36, 37, A

ROMANO

For a huge variety of shoes, boots and sandals for both men and women, Romano has perhaps the most comprehensive selection. You'll see trendy young Florentines trying on kitten heels next to little old ladies looking at shoes that you didn't think were made any more. Not too pricey, either.

🔳 F5 ⊠ Via Speziali 10r ☎ 055 216 535 🚌 A

SALVATORE FERRAGAMO

Designer shoes in the Palazzo Spini Feroni, which has a museum of shoes (▷ 38). Considered to be the leading brand in Italian shoes and bags.

🔳 E6 ⊠ Via de' Tornabuoni 16r ☎ 055 292 123 🚌 6, 11, 22, 36, 37, A

SISLEY

Italian Sisleys have a much wider selection of fashion than their British counterparts, and the prices are up to 30 per cent lower too. The Benetton subsidiary has a wide range of separates and accessories, as well as a number of the season's unmissable buys.

🔳 F5 ⊠ Via Roma (corner of Via Tosinghi) ☎ 055 286 669 🚌 A

SORBI

A kiosk in the middle of Piazza della Signoria now in its third generation of ownership, this is the very best place in Florence to buy postcards. Save yourself many a frustrating hour and come here first to look for postcards, particularly those of the great art in Florence's museums and churches.

🔳 F6 ⊠ Piazza della Signoria ☎ 055 294 554 🚌 A, B

VALLI

Fine dress fabrics as used by Dormeuil, Armani, Versace, Gianfranco Ferré and the like.

🔳 E6 ⊠ Via Strozzi 4–6r ☎ 055 282 485 🚌 6, 11, 22, 36, 37, A

VALMAR

A compact shop that sells trims and finishings for fashion and upholstery.

🔳 F6 ⊠ Via Porta Rossa 53r ☎ 055 284 493 🚌 6, 11, 36, 37, A

VANDA NENCIONI

Pretty gilded frames, as well as period and modern prints.

🔳 F6l ⊠ Via della Condotta 25r ☎ 055 215 345 🚌 A

VINARIUS

Sample a glass before you buy at this elegant enoteca; experts will help you make your selection. Also local extra virgin olive oil, balsamic vinegar, handmade pasta, mustards and delicacies made with truffles and honey.

🔳 G6 ⊠ Borgo Santa Croce 15r ☎ 055 200 1216 🚌 13, 23, B, C

CLOTHES SHOPPING

The most exclusive designers are in the district of Via de' Tornabuoni and Via della Vigna Nuova. The area around Piazza della Repubblica and Via dei Calzaiuoli has a good range of high-street clothes shops, including Max Mara and Marcella. In the streets east of Via dei Calzaiuoli there are many mid-range fashion boutiques. The areas around Santa Croce and San Lorenzo sell bargain fashions to the tourist market.

Entertainment and Nightlife

CAFFÈ MEGARA

At night this pleasing café in the elegant clothes shopping district turns into a bustling bar where you can sip cocktails into the early hours.

🔐 E5 ⊠ Via della Spada 11–17 ☎ 055 211 837
🚍 6, 11, 22, 36, 37, A

CHIESA DI SANTA MARIA DE RICCI

If you would like to sample the distinctive sound of Florentine organ music, then this is the place to visit. A wonderfully evocative setting in which to hear music similar to that head by Dante here in the 13th century.

🔐 F5 ⊠ Via del Corso ☎ 055 215 044
🚍 14, A

HARRY'S BAR

This American bar is one of the best places for elegant cocktails and it is as popular as ever. The food is international and very good; you can also get a good hamburger. The service is speedy and exemplary. Attractively placed on the banks of the River Arno.

🔐 D6 ⊠ Lungarno Vespucci 22r ☎ 055 239 6700
🕐 Closed Sun 🚍 A, B

H202

Drop in to this preclub bar, close to Santa Croce, where you can hear up-to-date clubby sounds.

🔐 G6 ⊠ Via Ghibellina 47r ☎ 055 243 239 🕐 Closed Wed 🚍 14

LIDO

This swanky bar along the River Arno has the feel of a colonial ship—you can even rent boats from here. Cocktails and innovative snacks are consumed while listening to to a sophisticated sound of lounge, drum and bass, and jazz beats.

🔐 J7 ⊠ Lungarno Pecori Giraldi 1 ☎ 055 234 2726
🕐 Closed Mon 🚍 12, 13, 14

LOONEES

This central friendly, studenty basement bar is popular with tourists and has occasional live music playing mainly British and American classic covers.

🔐 F6 ⊠ Via Porta Rossa 15 ☎ 055 212 249 🚍 6, 11, 36, 37, A

MAYDAY

Locals swarm around this stylish music bar where, into the early hours, you can indulge in a glass of

---

EVENING STROLL

Going out in Florence in the evening doesn't have to mean actually going anywhere. In summer a really enjoyable and popular way of spending time after dinner is to stroll through the streets of the historic section, stopping off for an ice cream or a drink at a bar. What's more is that you'll see plenty of groups of Italians of all ages and genders doing exactly the same thing.

---

wine, good beer or a cocktail while listening to quality live music. Very centrally located.

🔐 F6 ⊠ Via Dante Alighieri 16r ☎ 055 238 1290
🕐 Closed Sun 🚍 14, 23, A

PASZKOWSKI

Enjoy a drink or meal in the elegant, refined surroundings of Paszkowski while being serenaded by live music from the piano bar. In summer the orchestra plays outside on the piazza.

🔐 F5 ⊠ Piazza della Repubblica 6r ☎ 055 210 236
🚍 A

TEATRO VERDI

Culture has always played an important part in the life of Florence and the Teatgro Verdi was founded in 1854. The theatre puts on drama, ballet and opera from January to April. The excellent Orchestra Regionale Toscana play concerts here between December and May.

🔐 G6 ⊠ Via Ghibellina 99 ☎ 055 212 320 🚍 14, 23, A

YAB

This is one of Florence's most central club discos, which means it is often full of young visitors to the city. Music and fashions here are always up-to-the-date. The theatrical surroundings add to the overall atmosphere.

🔐 F6 ⊠ Via Sassetti 5r ☎ 055 215 160 🕐 Closed Wed 🚍 6, 22, A

ENTERTAINMENT AND NIGHTLIFE

THE SOUTH CENTRO

Restaurants

PRICES

Prices are approximate, based on a 3-course meal for one person.
€€€   over €45
€€   €20–€45
€   under €20

ALLE MURATE (€€€)

Sophisticated restaurant where traditional Tuscan cooking is given an innovative twist. Choose from beautifully prepared fish and meat dishes including turbot and duck. The soft lighting and candles make for an intimate dining experience.

➕ G6 ✉ Via Ghibellina 52r ☎ 055 240 618 🕐 Closed Mon, 2 weeks Aug 🚌 14, A

BALDOVINO (€€)

Bustling trattoria not far from Piazza Santa Croce. Especially good for those with children as they serve great pizza, from a wood burning oven, and the ambience is relaxed and not intimidating. The wide-ranging menu is constantly changing.

➕ H6 ✉ Via San Giuseppe 22r ☎ 055 241 773 🚌 14, C

BELLE DONNE (€–€€)

An inexpensive option in an expensive part of town. It's small, modest and you can barely see inside because of the potted plants. The menu has some interestingly prepared vegetables. You will probably share a table with others.

➕ E5 ✉ Via delle Belle Donne 16r ☎ 055 238 2609 🚌 36. 37, A

DA BENVENUTO (€)

There's lots of solid Tuscan food to choose from at this long-standing venue in the Santa Croce quarter.

➕ G6 ✉ Via della Mosca 16r ☎ 055 214 833 🕐 Closed Wed 🚌 23, B

BOCCADAMA (€€€)

Interesting food and good wine, plus views of the Basilica Santa Croce make this lively historic *enoteca* that doubles as a restaurant, very popular. You can eat on the delightful terrace, and there are more than 15 different wines uncorked for tasting sessions every evening.

ETIQUETTE

Italians have a strongly developed sense of how to behave, which applies in restaurants as much as anywhere else. It is bad form to order only one course in any restaurant (if that is what you want, go to a pizzeria). And the concept of a doggy bag could not be more at odds with Italian ideas of eating out. You might succeed in getting one, but you will pay a high price in the loss of dignity. Italians do not get drunk in public; to do so is to make a an appalling impression.

➕ G6 ✉ Piazza Santa Croce 25–26r ☎ 055 243 640 🚌 14, 23, C

LA BUSSOLO (€€)

La Bussolo serves some of the best pizza in town cooked in a traditional wood-burning oven; also good seafood dishes. In a rustic setting with a relaxed friendly service where you can eat from the bar.

➕ F6 ✉ Via Porta Rossa 58r ☎ 055 293 376 🚌 6, 11, 36, 37, A

CAFFÈ AMERINI (€€)

The Armerini lies in the main fashionable shopping area, and makes a good venue for taking a break during the day. Be warned though—it gets very popular in the early afternoon. Snacks and a variety of pastries packed with tasty fillings.

➕ E6 ✉ Via della Vigna Nuova 63r ☎ 055 284 941 🕐 Closed Sun 🚌 6, A

CANTINETTA DEI VERRAZZANO (€€)

A wonderful wine bar-cum-shop selling breads baked on the premises and wines from the Castello di Verrazzano estates near Greve. The marble-topped tables are both rustic and sophisticated, like the wines and food. Don't miss the *focaccia* (flat loaf), baked in the wood-burning ovens.

➕ F6 ✉ Via de' Tavolini 18–20r ☎ 055 268 590 🕐 Closed Sun 🚌 A

CAPOCACCIA (€)

This stylish café bar is one of the places to be seen in Florence. It's famous for its sumptuously filled panini and American-influenced brunch menu. Eat out in style in the frescoed salone or in the bar area overlooking the River Arno.

➕ E6 ✉ Lungarno Corsini 12–14r ☎ 055 210 751 🚌 B

IL CESTELLO (€€€)

Dine in style in a grand salon at the Westin Excelsior Hotel, with views of the River Arno. Here you will find a fusion of international haute cuisine and traditional Mediterranean and Tuscan influences. Only the finest seasonal ingredients are used. You get the chance to try specific cuisines such as from the Puglia region in the south.

➕ D5 ✉ Piazza Ognissanti 3 ☎ 055 271 51 🚌 6, 11, 36, 37, A, B, D

IL CIBREO (€€€)

This restaurant, one of the city's gastronomic shrines, offers no pasta but instead an intriguing range of robust Florentine dishes.

➕ H6 ✉ Via dei Macci 118r ☎ 055 234 1100 🕐 Closed Sun, Mon, Aug 🚌 A, C

COCO LEZZONE (€€€)

Popular with Florentines, with informal white-tile rooms. The short menu offers Tuscan classics.

➕ E6 ✉ Via del Parioncino 26r ☎ 055 287 178 🕐 Closed Tue dinner and Sun 🚌 6, A, B

COLLE BERETO (€€)

This new off-shoot of a Chianti wine producer offers quick but refined lunches from a Tuscan menu washed down by fine wine. Large picture windows, perspex chairs and black tables give a cool minimalist feel. Outside terrace.

➕ E6 ✉ Piazza Strozzi 5r ☎ 055 283 156 🚌 6, 22, A

EITO (€€–€€€)

A corner of Japan in Florence where beautifully presented, refined Japanese cooking attempts to arouse new sensations. The delightful ambience of this small restaurant creates a pleasant relaxing and intimate atmosphere.

BREAD

Almost all bread in Tuscany is made without salt. This takes some getting used to, but the blandness makes a good background to highly seasoned foods such as Florentine salami Finocchiona, which is scented with fennel and garlic. And the bread's texture–firm, almost coarse, and very substantial–is wonderful. Strict laws govern what goes into Italian bread: It is free of chemical preservatives.

➕ G6 ✉ V ia dei Neri 72r ☎ 055 210 940 🕐 Closed Mon 🚌 23, B, C

ENOTECA PINCHIORRI (€€€)

The city's most fashionable and priciest eatery is somewhat serious. For wine connoisseurs it is a must, possessing one of Europe's very finest wine cellars. Reserve ahead.

➕ G6 ✉ Via Ghibellina 87 ☎ 055 242 777 🕐 Closed Sun–Wed lunch, Aug 🚌 14, A

FESTIVAL DEL GELATO (€)

There are more than 80 different varieties of ice cream to choose from in this *gelataria*. It may not be the most celebrated but the ice cream on sale here is guaranteed to please. The fruit choices are particularly good.

➕ F5 ✉ Via del Corso 75r ☎ 055 294 386 🕐 Closed Mon 🚌 14, 23, A

GILLI (€€–€€€)

A chic, opulent café in the Piazza della Repubblica; the pastries are renowned (but pricey). Sit outside and indulge in, say, a lavish ice-cream sundae.

➕ F5 ✉ Piazza della Repubblica 39r ☎ 055 213 896 🕐 Closed Tue 🚌 6, A

GIUBBE ROSSE (€€–€€€)

This celebrated café was once the haunt of futurists and the Florentine

Trattoria

avanguardia scene. The red-jacketed waiters and stylish interiors hint at this illustrious past. Drink coffee and watch the world go by on the elegant Piazza Repubblica.

➕ F5 ✉ Piazza della Repubblica 13r ☎ 055 212 280 🚍 6, 22, A

GRAND HOTEL INCANTO (€€€)

The lavish interiors of this renovated grand hotel restaurant have a striking contemporary feel. A well-balanced menu; try the *gamberi* (prawns) and the fabulous desserts.

➕ D5 ✉ Piazza Ognissanti 1 ☎ 055 271 6767 🚍 A, B

HOSTARIA BIBENDUM (€€€)

Located in the Hotel Helvetia & Bristol, this restaurant and cocktail bar exudes exclusivity. Expect gilt, chandeliers, draperies and a formal atmosphere. Safe but expertly prepared menu.

➕ E5 ✉ Via dei Pescioni 2 ☎ 055 26651 🚍 6, 11, 22, 36, 37, A

IL LATINI (€€)

Boisterous restaurant offering Tuscan classics such as *pappardelle con la lepre* (wide strips of pasta with hare sauce). Other interesting dishes include wild boar *dolceforte* (wild boar stewed in honey, dried fruit and pinenut sauce). Seating is at communal tables.

➕ E5 ✉ Via dei Palchetti 6r ☎ 055 210 916 ⓒ Closed Mon 🚍 A, 6

IL MANDARINO (€€–€€€)

There are not a great deal of Chinese restaurants in the city and this one is centrally located..

➕ F6 ✉ Via della Condotta 17r ☎ 055 239 6130 ⓒ Closed Mon 🚍 A

OLIVIERO (€€€)

Excellent service, soft fabric-filled interiors and superb Tuscan food are the main characteristics of this eatery. Meat-lovers have a lot to choose from including wild boar, guinea fowl and rabbit. Sublime soups, exquisite vegetables and innovative pasta creations.

➕ E6 ✉ Via delle Terme 51r ☎ 055 287 643 ⓒ Closed Sun, Aug 🚍 6, 11, 36, A, B

PIZZA AT ITS BEST

As in every Italian town, pizzas are all over and many shops sell *pizza a taglio* (cut pizza). A good option for a quick snack is a slice. In addition to the standard margherita pizza (tomato and mozzarella), you will find all kinds of other delicious toppings, such as courgette (zucchini) flowers and aubergine (eggplant). Go when they're busy and the turnover is high to avoid eating cold pizza that's been sitting around for a while.

OSTERIA DE' BENCI (€)

A genuine Florentine *osteria*. Start with *crostini* (Tuscan *bruschetta*—toasted bread served with spreads, cheeses and cold meats) then choose from the day's menu that often includes spaghetti in red wine and/or a delicious vegetable soup. The meat is particularly good.

➕ G6 ✉ Via de' Benci 13 ☎ 055 234 4923 ⓒ Closed Sun, Aug 🚍 14, 23

PALLOTTINO (€€)

In business for nearly 100 years, this traditional trattoria has small dining rooms, wooden tables and candles. It is near Santa Croce and is known for its cheese and salami platters. Expect excellent pasta dishes.

➕ G6 ✉ Via Isola delle Stinche 1r ☎ 055 289 573 🚍 13, 23, B

PASZKOWSKI (€€–€€€)

Located on the grandiose Piazza della Repubblica, this is a lovely, if expensive, old-world café and tearoom where a piano bar adds a note of refinement to an already delightful interior.

➕ F5 ✉ Piazza della Repubblica 6r ☎ 055 210 236 🚍 6, 22, A

PERCHÉ NO! (€)

'Why not!' has to be a good name for an ice-cream place. Founded in 1939, this shop still

49

produces plenty of new tastes to discover and get excited about. For a taste of the Mediterranean try the Mezzogiorno preferred Malaga, which is dotted with rich wine grapes. It is renowned for its *semifreddi*, which come in creamy tastes such as hazelnut mousse and *zuppa inglese* (trifle). Perché No! is close to Piazza della Signoria.

➕ F6 ✉ Via dei Tavolini 19r ☎ 055 239 8969 🕓 Closed Tue 🚌 6, A

PERSEO (€)

Children and adults alike will be tantalized by the mountains of delicious ice cream on view. Try the fresh fruit tastes such as *fragola* (strawberry) and mango, which are all equally tempting and difficult to resist. Ideally placed for a refreshment break between museums and shopping shifts. Ice cream heaven.

➕ F6 ✉ Piazza della Signoria 16r 🕓 Closed Sun ☎ 055 239 8316 🚌 A, B

PILLORI D'ARNO (€)

The decor may be slightly functional, but the staff are very friendly in this local's café/bar in Ognissanti. Various assorted characters drift in and out consuming the excellent coffee, freshly squeezed orange juice, pastries and snacks.

➕ D5 ✉ Borgo Ognissanti 65r ☎ 055 292 195 🕓 Closed Mon 🚌 A, B, D

PROCACCI (€–€€)

Delightful bar that is something of a legend because of its panini tartufati, sandwiches made with a white truffle puree. This is just the thing to go with a glass of Tuscan wine at 11am.

➕ E5 ✉ Via de' Tornabuoni 64r ☎ 055 211 656 🚌 6, 11, 22, 36, 37, A

RIVOIRE (€€–€€€)

This café is a Florentine institution. At Rivoire, which opened in the 1870s, you pay for the view, but it's worth it. Looking out towards the Palazzo Vecchio, this is the ideal place to relax after a hectic visit to the Uffizi.

➕ F6 ✉ Piazza della Signoria 5r ☎ 055 214 412 🕓 Closed Mon, 2 weeks in Jan 🚌 A, B

ROSE'S (€)

A modern and sleek bar that serves great cocktails, but is also one of the few places in Florence where

> ### STAND OR SIT
>
> You will almost always pay a premium to sit down and to enjoy the privilege of waiter service at coffee shops, cafés and gelateria that often double up as all-round bars to be enjoyed during the day. If you stand, which is less expensive, you are generally not expected to linger too long after finishing your refreshment.

you can eat good sushi.

➕ E6 ✉ Via del Parione 26r ☎ 055 287 090 🕓 Closed Sun lunch 🚌 6, 11, 36, 37, A, B

TRATTORIA MARIONE (€)

Good home cooking based on simple, local ingredients. Well-prepared dishes include *bollito* (boiled beef), soups and tripe.

➕ E5 ✉ Via della Spada 27r ☎ 055 214 756 🚌 36, 37, A

TRATTORIA PONTE VECCHIO (€€–€€€)

A stone's throw from the Ponte Vecchio and its crowds, this trattoria is inevitably popular with visitors and you cannot fault the Tuscan cuisine. One of the house specials is pasta with mushrooms.

➕ F6 ✉ Lungarno Archibusieri 8r ☎ 055 292 289 🚌 D

VIVOLI (€)

Vivoli is legendary among foreign visitors. The family have been making ice cream since the 1930s, making it Florence's most famous *gelateria*. If you don't mind the wait, the rewards are delicious. Lots of choices, including an extra-creamy *mousse di amaretto*. All served in *coppette* (different-size cups); Vivoli is a no-cone zone.

➕ G6 ✉ Via Isola delle Stinche 7r ☎ 055 292 334 🕓 Closed Mon 🚌 14, 23, A

A district abundant with fine churches, the epitome of which is the magnificent Duomo.

2

3

VIALE FILIPPO STROZZI

Via del Pratello

V. C. Barbano

● Bett Ricasoli

Via F. Zanobi

Via Bartolommei

Palazzo dei Congressi

Piazza dell' Indipendenza

P

P

Via Ventisette

Via S. Reparata

Palazzo Affari

VIA

Ubaldio ● Peruzzi

V. della Fortezza

4

P

VALFONDA

Via B. Cennini

Via Nazionale

Via della Fortezza

Via Nazionale

Cenancolo di Foligno

Via Panicale

Via di Chiara

GUELFA

Ex Conv d S Apollonia

Bibliote Marucelli

Via Cimori

Via Orsola

P

i

Via Faenza

S Antonino d Lento

Mercato Centrale

Piazza d Merc Centr

Via Taddea

Borgo la Noce

Via del canto d Nelli

Via della stura

S GIOVAN

P

VIA

S MARIA NOVELLA

V. S. Cat. da Siena

LUIGI ALAMANNI

Obelisk dell' Unita d'Italia

Cappelle Medicee

t

Palazzo Medici-Ric

Teatro Re Toscano

Via

Via degli Alberi

VIA DELLA SCALA

Santa Maria Novella

V d Malarancio

Piazza dell' Unità Italiana

San Lorenzo

Biblioteca Laurenziana

Mercato San Lorenzo

Borgo S Lorenzo

V DE MARTELL

Via de Pu

Teatro Niccolini

M dell'O del Du

P

Via Palazzuolo

VIA PANZANI

Via del Giglio

Via dell' Alloro

Via de' Conti

Piazza Santa Maria Novella

V D BANCHI

V D RONDINELLI

VIA D CERRETANI

Battistero

Piazza d S Giovanni

Duomo

Piazza del Duomo

5

P

Via d Agli de'Pecori

Via Roma

Campanil

V d. Oche

6

7

0 ————————— 250 m

0 ————————— 250 yds

D   E   F

Via Salvestrini

Palazzo andolfini

CAVOUR

Via Pier

Via Chiarini

Piazza Isidoro dei Lungo

VIALE GIACOMO MATTEOTTI

Via L S

Via Ant

Via Dogana

Museo Botanico

Via Micheli

Via Venezia

Via Capponi

an Marco

Via S Giorgio la Costa

Giardino dei Semplici

Giardino della Gherardesca

azza Marco

Università

Palazzo Capponi

Via C Battisti

Santissima Annunziata

Via

Piazzale Donatello

PINTI

Cimitero degli Inglesi

alleria ell'Accademia

Piazza d Ss Annunziata

Ferdinando I

Via Laura

Museo Archeologico

Giuseppe

P

Via V Alfieri

VIALE ANTONIO GRAMSCI

tre di ardo

Piazza Brunelleschi

Via degli

Ospedale d Innocenti

BORGO

Via Laura

Palazzo Paneiatichi Ximenes

Giuste

Via P Giordani

Via S S

P

Via della Mattonaia

Via Capponi

Santa Maria Maddalena dei Pazzi

PINTI

Colonna

Piazza Massimo D'Azeglio

Ospedale Maria Nuova

Via della

Alfani

Crocifisso d Perugina

Via L C Farini

Via G B Niccolini

ini

Piazza S M Nuova

Teatro d Pergola

V C d Pergola

Via Fiesolana

Via della

Sinagoga

de Pilastri

Via G Carducci

V G Leopardi

i

Museo di Firenze com'era

ell'Oriuolo

BORGO

Via de Pepi

Via de Pepi

P

Museo Nazionale i Antropologia Etnologia

go d Albizi

Volta di S Piero

Piazza G Salvemini

Via Mezzo

Via Pietrapiana

Via della Mattonaia

G   H   J

The North Centro

Bronze panel from the 'Door of Paradise' by Pisano that decorates the Battistero

Battistero

Perhaps the most loved of all Florence's edifices is the beautiful octagonal Baptistery referred to by Dante as his 'bel San Giovanni', and dedicated to St. John the Baptist, the city's patron saint.

Roman origins The Baptistery is one of the oldest buildings in Florence: The remains of a Roman palace lie under it, and the dates given for the present construction vary between the 5th and the 7th centuries AD. For many centuries it was the place where Florentines were baptized and it is clear where the font stood until its removal in 1576.

Rich ornament The entire outer surface is covered with a beautiful design of white and green marble, added between the 11th and 13th centuries. Inside, the ceiling is encrusted with stunning mosaics: Above the altar, designs show the Virgin and St. John the Baptist; the main design shows the Last Judgement, with the sinful being devoured by diabolical creatures, while the virtuous ascend to heaven. Do not miss the tessellated floor, almost Islamic in its intricate geometry.

Bronze doors The Baptistery is renowned, above all, for its bronze doors: the south doors, by Pisano (1336), and Ghiberti's north and east doors (1403–24 and 1425–52). The east doors, referred to by Michelangelo as the 'Gates of Paradise', are divided into 10 panels depicting Old Testament scenes. In 1990 copies of these doors replaced the originals, which are on view in the Museo dell'Opera del Duomo (▷ 62).

THE BASICS

www.operaduomo.firenze.it
✚ F5
✉ Piazza San Giovanni
☎ 055 230 2885
🕐 Mon–Sat 12–7, Sun, hols 8.30–2
🚌 1, 14, 23, A
♿ Good
🎫 Moderate

HIGHLIGHTS

● 13th-century mosaics of the *Last Judgement*
● Ghiberti's east doors
● Pisano's south doors
● Zodiac pavement
● Romanesque marble exterior

Campanile

The superb bell tower affords fantastic views of the city—the climb is worth the effort

Tall, graceful and beautifully proportioned, the bell tower of the Duomo is one of the loveliest in Italy and adds a calm and graceful note to the otherwise busy cathedral complex.

Multiple effort The Campanile, or bell tower, of the Duomo stands 85m (279ft). It was begun in 1334 and completed in 1359. Giotto was involved in its design, but by the time of his death in 1337 only the base had been completed. Andrea Pisano completed the second floor and the tower was finished by Francesco Talenti.

Relief sculpture The outer surface is decorated in the same polychrome marble as the Duomo: white marble from Carrara, green marble from Prato and pink marble from the Maremma. Around the bottom are two sets of relief sculptures: The lower tier is in hexagonal panels, the upper tier in diamonds. What you see are in fact copies; the originals have been moved to the Museo dell'Opera del Duomo (▷ 62) to prevent further atmospheric damage. The reliefs in the hexagonal panels, which were executed by Pisano (although some are believed to have been designed by Giotto), show the Creation of Man, the Arts and the Industries. On the north face are the five Liberal Arts (grammar, philosophy, music, arithmetic and astrology), executed by Luca della Robbia. The upper tier of reliefs, also the work of Pisano, illustrates the Seven Planets, the Seven Virtues and the Liberal Arts; the Seven Sacraments are attributed to Alberto Arnoldi.

Maddona and Child by Michaelangelo (left). The Medici Chapels (right)

Cappelle Medicee

Of all the places in Florence associated with Michelangelo, the Medici Chapels, the mausoleum of the Medici family, are the most intriguing: with tomb sculptures, Madonna and Child, and sketches.

Burial places The mausoleum of the Medici family is in three distinct parts of the church of San Lorenzo (▷ 64): The crypt, the Cappella dei Principi and the Sagrestia Nuova. The crypt was where the bodies of minor members of the dynasty were unceremoniously dumped. Tidied up in the 19th century, it now houses tomb slabs. In the Cappella dei Principi is a huge dome by Bernado Buontalenti, begun in 1604 and not completed until the 20th century. The inner surface is decorated in a heavy, grandiose way that speaks of political tyranny: The Medici coat of arms is rarely out of view. The tombs of six Medici Grand Dukes are in the chapel beneath the dome.

New Sacristy Right of the altar, the Sagrestia Nuova, built by Michelangelo between 1520 and 1534, is a reminder that the Medici were enlightened patrons. Michelangelo sculpted figures representing *Night and Day*, and *Dawn and Dusk* to adorn the tombs of Lorenzo, Duke of Urbino (1492–1519), and Giuliano, Duke of Nemours (1479–1516). The figure of *Night*, with moon, owl and mask, is one of his finest works. The *Madonna and Child* (1521) is also by Michelangelo. In a room left of the altar are some superb charcoal drawings found in 1975 and attributed to Michelangelo.

THE BASICS

✚ F5
✉ Piazza Madonna degli Aldobrandini
☎ 055 238 8602
⏰ Daily 8.15–5, hols 8.15–1.50 (last admission 30 mins before closing); closed 1st, 3rd, 5th Mon, 2nd, 4th Sun of month and 1 Jan, 1 May, 25 Dec
🚌 1, 17, A
♿ Poor; ask for assistance
💶 Expensive
❓ English audio guides moderate

HIGHLIGHTS

● Michelangelo's *Night*
● The figure of Lorenzo, Duke of Urbino
● Michelangelo's *Madonna and Child*
● Sketches attributed to Michelangelo
● Charcoal drawings by Michelangelo

Duomo

HIGHLIGHTS

● Brunelleschi's dome
● Santa Reparata remains
● Uccello's mural to a 14th-century Captain-General

TIP

● You will not be allowed into the Duomo wearing skimpy shorts or a sleeveless top.

The famous dome of this cathedral dominates the Florence skyline, with its eight white ribs on a background of terracotta tiles. From close up, the size of the building is overwhelming.

Long-term build The cathedral of Santa Maria del Fiori, the Florence Duomo, is a vast Gothic structure built on the site of the 7th-century church of Santa Reparata, whose remains can be seen in the crypt. It was built at the end of the 13th century, although the colossal dome, which dominates the exterior, was not added until the 15th century, and the façade was not finished until the 19th century. The exterior is a decorative riot of pink, white and green marble; the interior is stark and plain. The clock above the entrance on the west wall inside was designed in 1443 by Paolo Uccello

Crowds gather beneath the Duomo (far left). The cupola is crowned by a lantern (middle). Intricate detail enhances the cathedral (right). Viewed from a height, the cupola is the glory of the Duomo (below left). The Last Judgement (below middle left). Detail inside the cathedral (below middle right). **Dante and his Worlds** *(below right)*

in accordance with the *ora italica*, according to which the 24th hour of the day ends at sunset.

Roman influences Built by Filippo Brunelleschi, who won the competition for its commission in 1418, the dome is egg-shaped and was made without scaffolding. Its herringbone brickwork was copied from the Pantheon in Rome. The best way to see the dome is to climb its 463 steps. The route takes you through the interior, where you can see Vasari's much-reviled frescoes of the *Last Judgement* (1572–79), and towards the lantern, from which the views are fantastic.

Explosion At Easter the *Scoppio del Carro*, a Mass-cum-theatrical pageant, ends with a mechanical dove being launched from the altar along a wire to the entrance, igniting a cart of fireworks.

THE BASICS

www.operaduomo.
firenze.it

✚ F5

✉ Piazza del Duomo

☎ 055 230 2885

🕐 Cathedral Mon–Fri 10–5, Sat 10–4.45 (1st Sat of month 10–3.30), Sun, hols 1.30–4.45.
Dome (access from south side of cathedral in Piazza del Duomo) Mon–Fri 8..30–7, Sat 8.30–5.40 (until 4 1st Sat of month)

🚌 1, 14, 23, A

♿ Good (access via Porta di Canonica (south side)

💶 Free; dome and crypt moderate

Galleria dell'Accademia

HIGHLIGHTS

- Michelangelo's *David*
- Michelangelo's *Prisoners*
- Giambologna's *Rape of the Sabine Women*
- Buonaguida's *Tree of Life*

TIP

- Go onto the website www.sbas.firenze/accademia where there is a floorplan to help you plan your visit.

Michelangelo's *David*, exhibited in the Accademia, has a powerful impact: the intensity of his gaze, that assured posture, those huge hands, the anatomical precision of the veins and the muscles.

Art School The Accademia was founded in 1784 to teach techniques of painting, drawing and sculpture. Since 1873 it has housed the world's single most important collection of sculptures by Michelangelo. There are also sculptures by other artists, as well as many paintings, mostly from the Renaissance period.

Masterpiece The main attraction is the *David* by Michelangelo, sculpted in 1504 and exhibited outside the Palazzo Vecchio until 1873, when it was transferred to the Accademia to protect it from

St. Francis Receiving the Stigmata, *an exhibit in the Galleria dell'Academia (left).*
The Tree of Life or Jesse's Tree by Pacino di Buonaguida is preserved in the gallery (middle). The most famous and most visited or all statues in Florence, the magnificent sculpture of David *by Michelangelo (right)*

environmental damage. It captures the moment at which the young David contemplates defying the giant Goliath. After controversial restoration techniques, David was unveiled in June 2004.

Freedom from stone The *Prisoners* (1505) were made for the tomb of Pope Julius II. The title refers to Michelangelo's belief that when he sculpted a statue, he was freeing the figure from the marble, and the style, particularly preferred by Michelangelo, was called the *non finito* (unfinished). After his death, the *Prisoners* were moved to the Grotta Grande in the Boboli Gardens (▷ 82), where the originals were replaced with casts in 1908. Also seek out the original plaster model for *The Rape of the Sabine Women* (1583), Giambologna's last work; the marble version is in the Loggia dei Lanzi in Piazza della Signoria (▷ 28).

THE BASICS

✚ G4
✉ Via Ricasoli 60
☎ 055 238 8609
🕐 Tue–Sun 8.15–6.50; closed 1 May
🚌 1, 7, 17, C
♿ Good
💷 Expensive

Museo dell'Opera del Duomo

TOP 25

Detail of a dancing choir by Lucca della Robbia (left). Striking displays (right)

THE BASICS

www.operaduomo.firenze.it
+ G5
⊠ Piazza del Duomo 9
☎ 055 230 2885
🕐 Daily 9–7.30
🚌 1, 14, 23
♿ Good
💰 Expensive

HIGHLIGHTS

● Choir lofts
● Original panels from the Campanile
● Michelangelo's *Pietà*
● Original panels from the 'Gates of Paradise'
● Donatello's *Maddalena*

There is something very pleasing about the idea of visiting the Cathedral Workshop, the maintenance section of the huge artistic undertaking that the cathedral complex represents.

Refuge from pollution This workshop-museum was founded when the Duomo was built, to maintain the art of the cathedral. Its location was chosen in the 15th century, and it was in its courtyard that Michelangelo sculpted his *David*. Since 1891 it has housed works removed from the cathedral complex, leaving the Duomo rather empty of art. It is also a refuge for outdoor sculptures.

Michelangelo's *Pietà* On the mezzanine levels you can see the construction materials and instruments used for Brunelleschi's dome, such as pulleys and brick moulds. On the main landing is the *Pietà* (begun c1550) by Michelangelo. It is said he intended it for his own tomb; the hooded figure of Nicodemus is often interpreted as a self-portrait. The damage to Christ's left leg and arm is believed to have been inflicted by Michelangelo in frustration at his failing skills.

Artists compared The main room on the first floor contains two choir lofts that once stood in the Duomo: one by Luca della Robbia (1431–38), the other by Donatello (1433–39). In the room on the left are reliefs by Pisano from the Campanile (▷ 56); in the final ground-floor room are eight of the original ten bronze panels from the east door of the Bapistery by Lorenzo Ghiberti.

Palazzo Medici-Riccardi

Opulence in the Palazzo Medici-Riccardi (left). Fresco by Luca Giordano (right)

The Medici family ruled with a mixture of tyranny and humanity, and this is reflected in the imposing façade of their huge headquarters, with its fearsome lattice of window bars.

Medici origins The Palazzo Medici-Riccardi, now mostly government offices, was the seat of the Medici family from its completion in 1444 until 1540, when Cosimo I moved the Medici residence to the Palazzo Vecchio and this palace was bought by the Riccardi family.

Setting a trend The palace, designed by Michelozzo, was widely imitated in Florence, for example in the Palazzo Strozzi and the Palazzo Pitti (▷ 84–85). It is characterized by huge slabs of stone, rusticated to give a roughly hewn rural appearance. The courtyard is in a lighter style, with a graceful colonnade and black and white *sgraffito* decoration of medallions, based on the designs of Roman intaglios collected by the Medici and displayed in the Museo degli Argenti (▷ 85).

A regal scene Steps right of the entrance lead to the Cappella dei Magi. This tiny chapel has the dazzling fresco cycle depicting the *Journey of the Magi* (1459–63) that Piero de' Medici commissioned from Gozzoli in memory of the Compagnia dei Magi, a religious organization to which the Medici belonged. Portraits of the Medici are believed to have been incorporated into the cast of characters, while the procession recalls the pageantry of the Compagnia dei Magi.

THE BASICS

www.palazzo-medici.it
✚ F5
✉ Via Cavour 3
☎ 055 276 0340
🕐 Thu–Tue 9–7
🚌 1, 7, 17
♿ Entrance on Via Cavour; Cappella poor
🎫 Cappella dei Magi moderate
❓ The Palazzo houses the Museo Mediceo, used for temporary exhibitions

HIGHLIGHTS

● Gozzoli's fresco cycle of the *Journey of the Magi* (1459–63)
● Compagnia dei Magi (Chapel of the Magi) with enchanting animals

San Lorenzo

The Basilica di San Lorenzo (left). The serene cloisters of San Lorenzo (right)

San Lorenzo is the parish church and burial place of the Medici and is filled with art commissioned by them. As with the Cappelle Medicee, it is a monument to the family's artistic patronage.

THE BASICS

- ✚ F5
- ✉ Piazza San Lorenzo
- ☎ 055 216 634
- 🕐 Mon–Sat 10–5
- 🚌 1, 11, 6, 17, A
- ♿ Poor
- 🎫 Inexpensive

HIGHLIGHTS

- Biblioteca Laurenziana (begun 1524)
- Staircase by Michelangelo
- Bronzino's *Martyrdom of St. Lawrence*
- Pulpits by Donatello
- Brunelleschi's Sagrestia Vecchia

A sacred site San Lorenzo was rebuilt by Filippo Brunelleschi 1425–46, on the site of one of the city's oldest churches (consecrated in AD393). Its rough-hewn ochre exterior was to have been covered with a façade by Michelangelo. This was never added, but a model is in Casa Buonarroti (▷ 37). The most bizarre piece of art here is the statue of Anna Maria Luisa (d1743), the last of the Medici dynasty, found—like a displaced Limoges porcelain figure—outside of the church. The church, with its *pietra serena* (grey sandstone) columns, is cool and airy. The bronze pulpits (c1460) depicting the Resurrection and scenes from the life of Christ are Donatello's last work. Bronzino's fresco (facing the altar, left) of the *Martyrdom of St. Lawrence* (1569) is an absorbing Mannerist study of the human body in various contortions. Inside Sagrestia Vecchia (Old Sacristy, 1421) are eight *tondi* (circular reliefs) by Donatello depicting the evangelists and scenes from the life of St. John.

Biblioteca Laurenziana The Laurentian Library (temporarily closed at time of writing) houses the Medici's collection of manuscripts (not on display). This extraordinary example of Mannerist architecture by Michelangelo is left of the church, up a curvaceous *pietra serena* staircase via the cloisters.

The Annunciation by Fra Angelico (left). The ornate exterior of San Marco (right)

San Marco

Dominated by the lovely paintings of Fra Angelico, the soothing convent of San Marco has an aura of monastic calm that is conducive to appreciating the religious themes depicted.

Medici motives San Marco was founded in the 13th century by Silvestrine monks. In 1437 Cosimo il Vecchio invited the Dominican monks of Fiesole to move into the convent and had it rebuilt by Michelozzo, a gesture motivated by his guilt for his wealth from banking and that the Dominicans were useful allies. Ironically, Savonarola, who denounced the decadence of the Medici at the end of the 15th century, came to prominence as the Dominican prior of San Marco.

A feast for the eyes The Chiostro di Sant' Antonino, the cloister through which you enter, is decorated with faded frescoes by Fra Angelico and other Florentine artists. In the Ospizio dei Pellegrini, where pilgrims were cared for, there is a superb collection of freestanding paintings by Fra Angelico and his followers. At the top of the stair-case on the way to the dormitory is Fra Angelico's *Annunciation* (1440), an image of great tender-ness and grace. Each of the 44 monks' cells is adorned with a small fresco by Fra Angelico or one of his assistants. The themes include the *Entombment* (cell 2) and the *Mocking of Christ* (cell 7). Savonarola's rooms house an exhibition about him. Cells 38 and 39 were reserved for Cosimo il Vecchio, who periodically spent time in the monastery.

THE BASICS

- ✚ G4
- ✉ Piazza San Marco 1
- ☎ 055 239 6950
- 🕐 Mon–Fri 8.30–1.50, Sat, Sun 8.30–7 (last admission 30 mins before closing); closed 1st, 3rd, 5th Sun, 2nd, 4th Mon of month
- 🚌 1, 6, 7, 10, 11, 17, 20, 25, 31, 32, 33, C
- ♿ Acceptable
- 💶 Moderate

HIGHLIGHTS

- ● Fra Angelico's cell paintings
- ● Fra Angelico's *Annunciation*
- ● Savonarola's cells
- ● Cosimo il Vecchio's cells

Santa Maria Novella

Santa Maria Novella's intricate façade makes an excellent perch for passing visitors

THE BASICS

www.smn.it

E5

Piazza di Santa Maria Novella

Church 055 215 918; Museum 055 282 187

Church Mon–Thu, Sat 9.30–5, Fri, Sun 1–5; closed during services. Museum Mon–Thu, Sat, Sun 9–5

5 mins walk from the railway station

A and all buses to train station

Good

Church inexpensive; museum inexpensive

HIGHLIGHTS

● Marble façade
● Masaccio's *Trinità*
● Cappellone degli Spagnoli, restored 2002
● Tornabuoni Chapel

The decorative marble façade of Tuscany's most important Gothic church incorporates billowing sails (emblem of Alberti's patron, Rucellai) and ostrich feathers (emblem of the Medici).

Dominican origins The church of Santa Maria Novella was built between 1279 and 1357 by Dominican monks. The lower part of the marble façade, Romanesque in style, is believed to be by Fra Jacopo Talenti; the upper part was completed between 1456 and 1470 by Leon Battista Alberti.

Deceptive interior Inside, the church is vast and looks even longer than it is, thanks to the clever spacing of the columns. As you face the altar, on the left-hand side is a fresco of the *Trinità* (c1428) by Masaccio, one of the earliest paintings to demonstrate mastery of perspective. Many of the chapels are named after the church's wealthy patrons. The Strozzi Chapel (left transept) is dedicated to St. Thomas Aquinas and decorated with frescoes (1351–57) by Nardo di Cione depicting *Heaven and Hell*: Dante himself is represented in the *Last Judgement* just behind the altar. The Tornabuoni Chapel contains Ghirlandaio's fresco cycle of the life of St. John the Baptist (1485) in contemporary costume. The Cappellone degli Spagnoli ('Spanish Chapel'), was used by the courtiers of Eleanor of Toledo, wife of Cosimo I. In the frescoes Triumph of the Doctrine (c1365) by Andrea da Firenze, the dogs of God (a pun on the word Dominican—*domini canes*) are sent to round up lost sheep into the fold of the church.

A scene from Life of Saint Benizzi (left) in Santissima Annunziata church (right)

Santissima Annunziata

The intimacy and delicate architecture of the Piazza della Santissima contrast with the grandeur of much of Florence. The roundels of babies on the Spedale degli Innocenti are quite enchanting.

Old New Year The Feast of the Annunciation on 25 March used to be New Year in the old Florentine calendar, and for that reason the church and the square have always played a special role in the life of the city. Every year, on 25 March, a fair is still held in the square and special biscuits called *brigidini* are sold.

Wedding flowers The church of Santissima Annunziata was built by Michelozzo in 1444–81 on the site of a Servite oratory. Entry is through an atrium known as the Chiostrino dei Voti (1447), which has the air of a rickety greenhouse though the frescoes inside are superb. They include Rosso Fiorentino's *Assumption*, Pontormo's *Visitation* and Andrea del Sarto's *Birth of the Virgin*. The church is dedicated to the Virgin Mary due to the legend that a painting of the Virgin was started by a monk in 1252 and finished by an angel. Newlyweds have traditionally brought their wedding bouquet to the church to ensure a happy marriage.

Early orphanage The Spedale degli Innocenti, on the east side of the piazza, was the first orphanage in Europe; part of the building is still used for the purpose, and UNICEF has offices here. Designed by Brunelleschi in 1419, it has enamelled terracotta roundels by della Robbia (1498).

THE BASICS

☖ G4
✉ Piazza della Santissima Annunziata
☎ 055 239 8034. Spedale degli Innocenti 055 203 7323
◷ Daily 7.30–12.30, 4–6.30; closed during services. Spedale Mon, Tue, Thu–Sun 8.30–2
🚍 6, C
♿ Good
💰 Free to church; moderate to Spedale

HIGHLIGHTS

● Andrea della Robbia's roundels
● Façade of the Spedale degli Innocenti
● Rosso Fiorentino's *Assumption*
● Pontormo's *Visitation*
● Andrea del Sarto's *Birth of the Virgin*

More to See

GIARDINO DEI SEMPLICI

This oasis of neat greenery, the botanical garden of Florence University, is on the site of a garden laid out in 1545–46 for Cosimo I, who wanted to keep up with the Pisans and Genoans. It is named after the medicinal plants (*semplici*) grown here. There are also greenhouses with tropical palms, orchids and citrus fruits.

⊞ G4 ⊠ Via Micheli 3 🕐 Daily 9–1, Sat 9–5; closed Wed 🚌 1, 7, 25 🔸 Good ✋ Moderate

MERCATO CENTRALE

The largest of Florence's produce markets is held in the magnificent cast-iron structure of the Mercato Centrale, built in 1874, with an extra floor added in 1980. Just about every kind of fresh food is sold here.

⊞ F4 ⊠ Piazza Mercato Centrale 🕐 Mon–Sat 7–2 (also Sep–end Jun Sat 4–8) 🍴 Yes 🚌 4, 12, 25, 31, 32 🔸 Good (but crowded)

MERCATO SAN LORENZO

Fun, touristy and centrally located in the shadow of the church of San Lorenzo. Lots of stalls sell leather goods, many of which are genuinely good value, but go armed with a healthy scepticism.

⊞ F5 ⊠ Piazza San Lorenzo 🕐 Apr–end Oct daily 9–8; Nov–end Mar Tue–Sun 9–7.30; closed Sun, Mon in winter 🍴 Yes 🚌 1, 17 🔸 Good

MOSTRE DI LEONARDO

This exhibition complex is dedicated to the 'genius of Leonardo' and displays some 40 models of the great man's inventions. Visitors are encouraged to touch and manoeuvre the machines, which have been reconstructed in wood, metal and textiles.

⊞ G5 ⊠ Via dei Servi 66–68 ☎ 055 282 966 🕐 Daily 10–7 🚌 C 🔸 Good ✋ Moderate

MUSEO ARCHEOLOGICO

One of the best places to see Etruscan art. There are also Roman, Greek and Egyptian exhibits. Be sure to see the rare collection from Kafiri, north Pakistan.

Artichokes for sale in the Mercato Centrale

☩ H4 ✉ Palazzo della Crocetta, Via della Colonna 36 ☎ 055 23575 🕐 Mon 2–7, Tue, Thu 8.30–7, Wed, Fri–Sun 8.30–2 🚌 6, C ♿ Good 💶 Moderate

MUSEO BOTANICO

www.unifi.it

A collection of the University of Florence, the museum, founded in 1842, houses 4 million specimens. It's the largest and most important collection of its kind in Italy. Don't miss the Andrea Cesalpino Herbarium and the wax models of plants.

☩ G3 ✉ Via La Pira 4 ☎ 055 275 7462 🕐 By appointment only; call first 🚌 1, 7, 25 ♿ Good 💶 Free

MUSEO DI FIRENZE COM'ERA

Paintings and maps showing how Florence was from the late 15th until the early 20th centuries. There's also 16th-century lunettes of the Medici villas, and the Pianta della Catena, an 1887 copy of a 1470 view of Florence.

☩ G5 ✉ Via dell'Oriuolo 24 ☎ 055 261 6545 🕐 Fri–Wed 9–2 🚌 14, 23, A ♿ Good 💶 Inexpensive

MUSEO NAZIONALE DI ANTROPOLOGIA E ETNOLOGIA

Founded in 1869, this museum offers something more than art and history. The people of the areas of Africa that came under Italian colonial rule are well represented.

☩ G5 ✉ Palazzo Nonfinito, Via del Proconsolo 12 ☎ 055 239 6449 🕐 Wed–Mon 9–1 🚌 14, 23 ♿ Good 💶 Moderate

SANTA MARIA MADDALENA DEI PAZZI

Although the original church dates from the 13th century, most of the present building is a Renaissance rebuild designed by Guiliano da Sangallo at the end of the 15th century. The spectacular interior decoration, with its marble and *trompe l'oeil*, dates from the baroque. The highlight here, however, is in the fresco of the 1490s by Perugino in the chapter house (reached via the crypt).

☩ H5 ✉ Borgo Pinti 58 🕐 Mon–Sat 9–12, 4.45–5.20, 6.15–6.50, Sun 9–10.45, 5–6.50 🚌 6, C ♿ Poor 💶 Inexpensive

Trompe l'oeil *in Santa Maria Maddalena dei Pazzi*

Entrance to the Museo Nazionale di Antropolgia e Ethnolgia

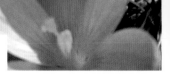

North of the City

Taking in Florence's main market area and the most important churches and galleries in the northern part of the city.

DISTANCE: 3km (2 miles) **ALLOW:** Full morning

START

CAPPELLE MEDICEE (▷ 57)
🚇 F5 🚌 1, 17, A

END

SANTISSIMA ANNUNZIATA (▷ 67)
🚇 G4 🚌 6, C

① Start at the Cappelle Medicee (▷ 57), in Piazza Madonna degli Aldobrandini, the last resting place of many of the Medici family.

② The church of San Lorenzo (▷ 64) itself (entered from Piazza San Lorenzo) is a masterpiece of Renaissance church design. Inside are works by Donatello.

③ Explore the market north of San Lorenzo; cut through the Mercato Centrale (▷ 68) and return to Piazza San Lorenzo. The Pallazzo Medici-Riccardi (▷ 63) is on the north side.

④ Follow Via Cavour, Via degli Alfani, Via San Reparata and Via XXVII Aprile to reach the former convent of Sant' Apollonia, with a fresco of the *Last Supper* by Andrea del Castagno.

⑧ Across the square is the Ospedale degli Innocent. If time permits go inside to see the modest museum and the two Brunelleschi cloisters.

⑦ This is one of the city's most distinctive squares. The square's church, Santissima Annunziata (▷ 67), is known for its frescoes by Andrea del Santo and others.

⑥ The ex-convent on the north side of the square houses Museo di San Marco (▷ 65), devoted to the frescoes and painting of Fra Angelico. Continue eastward to Piazza della Santissima Annunziata.

⑤ Walk east to Piazza San Marco, pausing to view Michelangelo's *David* in the Galleria dell'Accademia (▷ 60–61)

Shopping

ABACUS
The sign on the door says that this bookbindery aspires to 'sturdiness and beauty'. The hand-stitched spines and exquisitely lined covers make the volumes exceptional gifts. For such good quality, the prices are surprisingly low.
🞜 F4 ✉ Via de'Ginori 28–30r ☎ 055 219 719 🚌 1, 6, 7, 10

ALICE'S MASKS ART STUDIO
Papier-mâché in all shapes and sizes are here: animals—mythical and real—as well as more theatrical and surreal characters. They are all hand painted and finished, making great gifts or wall hangings.
🞜 E4 ✉ Via Faenza 72r ☎ 055 287 350 🚌 4, 12, 25, 31, 32, 33

ARTE CRETA
Admire artist Elisabetta di Costanzo painting her majolica fresh from the kiln in brilliant hues. Her delightful pieces make a refreshing souvenir.
🞜 G6 ✉ Via del Proconsolo 63r ☎ 055 284 341 🚌 14, 23, A

BALLOON
This Italian chain sells funky casual clothing that looks good on all generations, made from natural fabrics such as silk and cotton.
🞜 G5 ✉ Via del Proconsolo 69r ☎ 055 212 460 🚌 A, 14, 23

BARTOLINI
A Florentine institution; the junction where it stands is referred to as 'Bartolini corner'. It sells just about every item of kitchenware you could wish for, as well as fine china and porcelain. All the worldwide names are here but look out for the Italian ceramics such as Italian Ars and Solimene-Vietri ware.
🞜 G5 ✉ Via dei Servi 30 ☎ 055 211 895 🚌 14, 23, C

BORGO
This small, tempting and well-stocked wine shop focuses on smaller local winemakers. Cheryl, the American lady who runs the shop with her Italian husband, is a font of knowledge. Also *biscotti,* pasta and olive oil.
🞜 E5 ✉ Borgo San Lorenzo ☎ 055 215 103 🚌 1, 6, 7, 10, 11, 14

BOTTEGA ORAFA PENKO
Master goldsmith Paolo Penco makes jewellery to order using techniques

---

MARBLED PAPER

The skill of marbling paper was brought to Florence from Venice, where it had been learned from the East in the 12th century. Today's Florentine paper goods range greatly in price and quality, but even the inexpensive goods are attractive—and easily transported.

---

from the Renaissance.
🞜 F5 ✉ Via F Zannetti 14 ☎ 055 211 661 🚌 1, 6, 11, A

LA BOTTEGHINA DEL CERAMISTA
The vivid and lively patterns that are hand painted on these jugs, bowls and dishes will brighten any table.
🞜 F4 ✉ Via Guelfa 5r ☎ 055 287 367 🚌 1, 6, 7, 10, 11, 17

CAFÉ DO BRASIL
Florentines come here to buy loose tea and to stock up on the freshly roasted Brazilian coffee. You can also choose from a wonderful selection of locally made jams, cookies, sauces and traditional sweets (candies) to take home.
🞜 G5 ✉ Via de Servi 89r ☎ 055 214 452 🚌 C, 6, 31, 32

CASA DEL VINO
This wine shop has occupied the same premises since it opened in the second half of the 19th century. Today it has a very well-stocked cellar with nearly 1,000 wines from around the world. You can try wine by the glass and have a snack while making a decision.
🞜 F4 ✉ Via dell'Ariento 16r ☎ 055 215 609 🚌 4, 12, 25, 31, 32

ECHO
It's doubtful you'll have ever heard of any of the labels in this shop but

you're sure to be bowled over by the clever designs. Go through the rails and check out the reasonable prices. A younger, funkier Echo is located nexr door.

⊞ G5 ⊠ Via dell' Orinolo 37r ☎ 055 238 1149 🚌 14, 23

EMPORIUM

These ceramics and items for the home may come from Provence, but their rustic appeal suits the Tuscans just fine.

⊞ E4 ⊠ Via Faenza 23–25r 1 ☎ 055 282 058 🚌 4, 12, 25, 33, 80

ERMENI

This bizarre fabric shop seems stuck in a time warp, but so long as you are serious about buying, it's worth visiting for some good value linen. There are also some more lavish fabrics for upholstering and soft furnishings.

⊞ F5 ⊠ Via Borgo San Lorenzo 3r ☎ 055 292 200 🚌 1, 6, 7, 10, 11, 14, 17, 23

FRATELLI ALINARI

For the kind of postcards you want to keep rather than send, Alinari's, established in 1852, has an awesome archive that includes some of the first photographs ever taken in Italy. You can order any print for a very reasonable price. It also sells beautiful coffee-table books.

⊞ E5 ⊠ Largo Alinari 15 ☎ 055 231 951 🚌 4, 12, 25

FRETTE

This world-famous Italian company produces refined superior fabrics for the home, always at the cutting edge of fashion; bedding, tableware and lots more.

⊞ G4 ⊠ Via Cavour 2 ☎ 055 211 369 🚌 A

HERMÈS

The biggest and best-equipped branch in Italy of the classically elegant Paris-based designer.

⊞ E5 ⊠ Piazza Antinori 6r ☎ 055 238 1003 🚌 6, 11, 22, 36, 37, A

INTIMISSIMI

The simple cotton and silk lingerie and sleep-wear is hard to beat in terms of quality and price. You can be assured a good service.

⊞ F5 ⊠ Via de Cerretani 15r ☎ 055 230 2609 🚌 1, 6, 7, 10, 11, 14, 17, 23

HOLY WINE

Trebbiano and Malvasia grapes are used to make *vin santo* (holy wine), which has a concentrated flavour and is about 14 per cent alcohol by volume. The grapes are semi-dried and made into wine, which is aged in small barrels for a number of years before bottling. It is drunk as a dessert wine—sometimes instead of dessert, when you use it to dunk hard, dry *biscotti di Prato* (also known as *cantuccini*).

I SAPORI DEL CHIANTI

A pretty shop with an wide range of wines, including first-class Chianti.

⊞ G5 ⊠ Via dei Servi 10r ☎ 055 238 2071 🚌 14, 23

LORETTA CAPONI

Deliciously feminine linens, nightclothes and lingerie for mother and daughter.

⊞ E5 ⊠ Piazza Antinori 4r ☎ 055 211 074 🚌 6, 11, 22, 23, 36, 37, A

MAXMARA

Classic elegance takes precedence over ostentation; clothes are of superb quality and beautifully tailored—yet at reasonable prices.

⊞ F5 ⊠ Via dei Pecori 23r ☎ 055 287 761 🚌 A

ORNAMENTA

This little shop sells small amber rings and silver earrings along with more ethnic styles at reasonable prices.

⊞ G5 ⊠ Via Proconsolo 65 ☎ 055 292 879 🚌 14, 23, A

PAPERBACK EXCHANGE

A wide selection of art and history books, both new and second-hand, are sold here. Trade in any books you've already read and take your pick from the out-of-print ones, including some in English.

⊞ F5 ⊠ Via delle Oche 4r ☎ 055 265 8395 🚌 14, 23, A

PASSAMANERIA TOSCANA FIRENZE

This shop sells a full range of furnishing fabrics, brocades, tassels and other trimmings as well as finished goods such as cushions and footstools. The shades and textures are rich and sensuous, the whole experience bordering on the utterly abandoned.

🔲 F5 ✉ Piazza San Lorenzo 12r ☎ Fax 055 214 670 🚌 1, 11, 6, 17, A

IL PAPIRO

These shops in central Florence sell excellent marbled paper goods in particularly pretty shades. These include little chests of drawers and tiny jewellery boxes.

🔲 G4 ✉ Via Cavour 55r ☎ 055 215 262; Piazza del Duomo 24r ☎ 055 281 628; 🔲 F6 ✉ Lungarno Acciaiuoli 42r ☎ 055 264 5613 🚌 1, 7, 17; 🔲 F6 ✉ Via dei Tavolini 13r ☎ 055 213 823 🚌 A

LE PIETRE NELL'ARTE

A really classy shop run by the Scarpelli family. They sell beautiful hard and semi-precious stone inlays, interior decorations and artistic objects including sculptures, tables, pictures, brooches and much more. The stones used included onyx, chalcedony, malachite and jasper.

🔲 F5 ✉ Piazza Duomo 36r ☎ 055 212 587 🚌 4, 12, 25, 31, 32

QUELLE TRE

While some of the clothes border on the bohemian, the wealth of textures, shades and shapes make this shop a superb find for quirky dressers.

🔲 F5 ✉ Via dei Pucci 43r ☎ 055 293 284 🚌 1, 6, 14

RICHARD GINORI

Florence's own porcelain designer. Also does dinner services to order with your family crest, a picture of your home or whatever else you want.

🔲 E5 ✉ Via Rondinelli 17r ☎ 055 210 041 🚌 6, 11, A

SCRIPTORIUM

This shop draws on two great Florentine crafts—leather working and papermaking—to create objects of great beauty and refined taste that are almost too beautiful to be used. The plain paper books are notable, bound with exquisitely soft leather in subdued natural shades.

🔲 G5 ✉ Via dei Servi 5r ☎ 055 211 804 🚌 14, 23, C

SGIBOLI TERRACOTTE

Pots here are designed, painted and fired in Florence by the family owners. The delightful designs for house and garden come in majolica and tactile unglazed terracotta and at very good prices.

🔲 G5 ✉ Via Sant'Egidio 4r ☎ 055 247 9713 🚌 14, 23

ZANOBINI

Part traditional bar, part wine shop, Zanobini's is patronzied by locals. Stop for a drink and a snack, and buy some good wine.

🔲 F4 ✉ Via Sant'Antonino 47r ☎ 055 239 6850 🚌 A

ZINI

Zini stocks Italy's most up-and-coming designers. The tailoring and cut of the clothes is impressive, and orginality comes in the interesting use of different prints and fabrics

🔲 F5 ✉ 26 Borgo San Lorenzo 20r ☎ 055 289 850 🚌 A

CHIANTI

Chianti gets its name from the region in which it is made. Sangiovese grapes are harvested in October, pressed and then the juice and skins of the grapes are fermented for about 15 days, after which the juice alone is given a second fermentation. In spring the wine is matured in wooden casks. *Chianti Classico* is usually regarded as the best of the seven types of Chianti. This is produced in the eponymous region north of Siena. Wines of the Chianti Classico Consortium bear the symbol of the Gallo Nero (black cockerel).

Entertainment and Nightlife

ASTOR CAFFÉ

Stylish café/bar near the Duomo serves up Mediterranean dishes accompanied by a house, jazz and easy-listening soundtrack. Grab a seat for an *apertivo* and munch on the buffet snacks before the DJ sets and occasional live music get going in the back room.

➕ F5 ✉ Piazza Duomo 20r ☎ 055 239 9000 🚌 1, 6, 7, 10, 11, 14, 17, 23, A

CHIESA DI SANTA MARIA DE'RICCI CONCERTI

If you would like to sample the distinctive sound of Florentine organ music, then this is the place to visit. A wonderfully evocative setting in which to hear music similar to that heard by Dante here in the 13th century.

➕ F5 ✉ Via del Corso ☎ 055 215 044 🚌 14, A

JAZZ CLUB

Another very popular venue among real jazz aficionados. Although technically a private club, it is very easy to become a member (▷ panel). If you like live jazz and a relaxed atmosphere, then this is the place for you.

➕ H5 ✉ Via Nuova dei Caccini 3 ☎ 055 247 9700 🚌 C

MARACANA

Six levels, a carnival stage and a party crowd make this lively club popular with lovers of all things Brazilian. Samba, sip caipirinhas and try churrasco chunks of meat.

➕ E4 ✉ Via Faenza 4 🌑 Closed Mon ☎ 055 210 298 🚌 4, 12, 25

REX CAFFÈ

A popular bar with a spellbinding interior of retro lighting and paint-splashed walls. An array of drinks from around the world include *mojitos* and daiquiris. Open until 2.30am.

➕ H5 ✉ Via Fiesolana 53r ☎ 055 248 0331 🚌 14, 23, A

CLUBS ITALIAN STYLE

Many clubs and music venues (and even a few bars and restaurants) are private clubs or *associazione culturale*. This doesn't mean that visitors are unwelcome but rather that it's easier for them to get a licence as a club than as a public *locale*. It's really very easy to become a member; you may be charged a euro or so over and above the official entry price, but it's still worth doing even if you're only going to use your membership once. Many clubs actually have free membership. All you need to do is fill in your name, address, date of birth and sometimes occupation on a form and you'll be presented with a membership card.

SPACE ELECTRONIC

Upstairs you'll find a vast dance floor, where a huge variety of music is played, from up-to-the-minute hits to 1950s and 60s classics. Noisy and very popular with tourists.

➕ D5 ✉ Via Palazzuolo 37 ☎ 055 293 457 🚌 36, 37, D

TEATRO COMUNALE

The largest of Florence's concert halls—the main venue of the Maggio Musicale and the festival's box office—also has its own classical season from mid-September to December. The opera season then begins, finishing mid-January and from then until April symphony concerts are held. The Ridotto or Piccolo is the theatre's smaller auditorium.

➕ C5 ✉ Corso Italia 16 ☎ Box office 055 213 535 🚌 B

TEATRO DELLA PERGOLA

Well-known theatre productions are regularly held in these sumptuous surroundings of the two elegant halls. This is an important venue for classical music in Florence, with some Maggio Musicale and Estate Fiesolana concerts held here. From October to April the Amici della Musica organize Saturday afternoon concerts here.

➕ G5 ✉ Via della Pergola 18/32 ☎ 055 247 9651 🚌 14, 23, C

Restaurants

PRICES

Prices are approximate, based on a 3-course meal for one person.

€€€	over €45
€€	€20–€45
€	under €20

BELCORE (€€)

One of Florence's newest spots where you can enjoy refined modern Italian cooking in tranquil, elegant surroundings. The plain cream walls provide a stage for the work of up-and-coming artists. There is an impressive wine list with more than 300 wines to choose from.

➕ D5 ✉ Via dell'Albero 30 ☎ 055 211 198 🕐 Closed lunch Tue, Wed 🚌 1, 2, 9, 16 17, A

CANTINETTA ANTINORI (€€€)

A refined setting for the chic Florentine elite. The food comes from the farm of the Antinori family, whose wines are world renowned. The wonderful dishes use the best seasonal produce: *bruschetta* (garlic toast), port, truffles, salted fish, hearty soups and pâté dominate in winter, and lighter pasta dishes, imaginative salads and fresh fish in warmer months. Dress up or you are likely to feel completely out of place.

➕ E5 ✉ Piazza Antinori 3 ☎ 055 292 234 🕐 Closed Sat, Sun, Aug 🚌 6, 11, 37, A

COQUINARIUS (€€)

This restaurant-cum-wine bar full of dark wood and stylish posters is a great place to sample lots of different cheeses, cold cuts, smoked fish, *carpacci* meats and *stuzzichini* (Italian bar snacks). Also soups and salads.

➕ F5 ✉ Via delle Oche 15r ☎ 055 230 2153 🕐 Closed Sun, Aug 🚌 14, 23, A

GELATERIA CARABÉ (€)

A top-quality Sicilian ice cream store run with tremendous pride by Antonio and Loredana Lisciandro. Gelateria Carabé is *the* place to have a *granita* (ice slush) in Florence—choose from lemon, coffee, fig, watermelon or even prickly pear. The pistachio *gelato* is outstanding. Near the Accademia, it's a rare treat not to be missed.

➕ G4 ✉ Via Ricasoli 60r ☎ 055 289 476 🚌 1, 6, 11, 17, C

GOZZI SERGIO (€)

A basic but good trattoria with a different menu every day. Hidden behind the Mercato San Lorenzo, it is not the easiest place to find and it's open only for lunch, but it's worth a detour.

➕ F5 ✉ Piazza San Lorenzo 8r ☎ 055 281 941 🕐 Closed dinner Sun, Aug 🚌 1, 17

LE MOSSACCE (€–€€)

Bustling eatery between the Duomo and the Bargello. Serves excellent Tuscan food including rich soup.

➕ G6 ✉ Via del Proconsolo 55r ☎ 055 294 361 🕐 Closed Sat, Sun, Aug 🚌 14, 23, A

ITALIAN CAKES

There are three main types of Italian cake. *Brioche* (pastries) are made with sweet yeast dough and filled with oozing custard. *Torte* (cakes) tend to be tarts, such as the ubiquitous *torta della nonna* (granny's cake), a kind of cake in tart form, or *torta di ricotta*, in which ricotta is mixed with sugar and candied peel. Then there are all kinds of little cookies, most of which contain nuts and have names like *brutti ma buoni* (ugly but good).

PALLE D'ORO (€)

Spotless and spartan, this restaurant serves good food and is excellent value. Expect hearty soups, gnocchi dumpling dishes, decent fish and filling pasta servings. Adequate wine list.

➕ F4 ✉ Via Sant'Antonino 43r ☎ 055 288 383 🕐 Closed Sun 🚌 1, 7, 10

RELAIS LE JARDIN (€€€)

The dark wood and carpeted interiors, and the lush well-kept gardens give the Hotel Regency's restaurant a British feel.

Immaculately prepared and presented menu. Reserve early to ensure a candlelit table.

⊞ H5 ⊠ Piazza Massimo D'Azeglio ☎ 055 245 247 ⊟ 6, 31, 32, C

ROBIGLIO (€€)

The old-fashioned Florentine bar/*pasticceria* par excellence opened its first branch in 1928. The pastries are to die for. Both these branches are closed Sunday.

⊞ F5 ⊠ Via Tosinghi 11r ☎ 055 215 013 ⊟ A; ⊞ G4 ⊠ Via dei Servi 112 ☎ 055 214 501 ⊟ 14, 23, C

RUTH'S (€)

A bright, modern eatery next to the synagogue serving an interesting mix of vegetarian (although fish is also served), Middle Eastern and kosher food.

⊞ H5 ⊠ Via Farini 2a ☎ 055 248 0888 ⓘ Closed Fri dinner, Sat lunch ⊟ A, C

SABATINI (€€€)

This elegant, wood-filled restaurant is a respected Florentine stalwart. Particularly good for local steak and excellent seafood risotto.

⊞ E5 ⊠ Via dei Panzani 9a ☎ 055 282 802 ⓘ Closed Mon ⊟ 1, 7, 11, 22, 36, 37, A

TAVERNA DEL BRONZINO (€€–€€€)

Here you will find a wealth of Tuscan culinary delights. Many have an international sparkle, including the deep-fried lamb chops served with vegetables. If available, and you love fish, try the expertly prepared sea bass.

⊞ F3 ⊠ Via delle Route 25r ☎ 055 495 220 ⓘ Closed Mon lunch, Sun, Aug ⊟ 12, 80

TRATTORIA ANTELLESI

A great place for a vegetarian to join a meat-eating friend. Good range of inventive salad starters and a delicious main course artichoke risotto. There is a decent wine list and nice pannacotta with *frutti del bosco* (fruits of the forest). The chestnut pudding is certainly different.

⊞ E4 ⊠ Via Faenza 9r ☎ 055 216 990 ⓘ Closed Tue ⊟ 4, 12, 25, 31, 32

TRATTORIA ANTICHI CANCELLI (€)

Hearty Tuscan food served at this mainstay trattoria. There is a good selection for vegetarians on the mixed menu, including hearty soups, *contorni* (side dishes) and the classic spaghetti *pomodoro e basilico* (tomato and basil). Good value house wine.

⊞ E4 ⊠ Via Faenza 73r ☎ 055 218 927 ⓘ Closed Mon ⊟ 4, 12, 25, 31, 32

IL VEGETARIANO (€)

A rare breed in Florence, this cafeteria-style space provides an inexpensive treat for vegetarians. Select from classic vegetarian fare posted on blackboards and eat at communal wood tables or outside in the courtyard. Excellent salads.

⊞ F3 ⊠ Via delle Route 30r ☎ 055 475 030 ⓘ Closed Sat and Sun lunch, Mon ⊟ 12, 80

ZÀ-ZÀ (€–€€)

An old-fashioned, inexpensive trattoria near the Mercato Centrale, which is very popular with visitors. The Tuscan food is excellent, and the fixed-price menus are great value. The inviting stone-walled interior is especially appealing in the summer heat. It's best to arrive at opening time or reserve a table.

⊞ F4 ⊠ Piazza del Mercato Centrale 26r ☎ 055 215 411 ⊟ 1, 6, 7, 10, 12, 25

Literally translated as 'beyond the Arno', the Oltrano is the site of the Pitti Palace and the Boboli Gardens. It is also the most relaxed part of the city, least touched by tourism and with some of the best views.

4

5

6

Piazza
di Cestello
San Frediano
LUNGARNO SODERINI
Piazza
N Sauro
Cest
LUNGARNO GUICCIARDINI
BOR SAN FREDIANO
Chiesa
S Presb
Piazza
di Presb
Palazzo
Frescobaldi
Piazza
di Frescobaldi
Via del Leone
Piazza del
Carmine
Borgo d Stella
SERRAGLI
Via
S Spirito
Spirito Frescobaldi
**Cappella
Brancacci**
S
Monaca
S SPIRITO
Via
Borgo
S Jacopo
Santa Maria
del Carmine
Via dell'Ardiglione
**Santo
Spirito**
Casa
Ridolfi
Palazzo
Frescobaldi
Via de' Guicciardini
Piazza
di Felicità
Piazza
di Rossi
**Santa
Felicità**
S
Via
della
Via de Bardi
de Mag
Pia
di S

7

VIALE
FRANCESCO
PETRARCA
*Giardino
Torrigiani*
Via
della
Chiesa
Campuccio
Via Santa Maria
Via S Agostino
Piazza
S Spirito
Mazzetta
Via Presso S Marino
Via
Romana
Via Maggio
Via
Sguazza
Palazzo
Corsini
Piazza
de' Pitti
**Galleria del
Costume**
**Palazzo
Pitti**
San
Girolamo
Santo
Spirito
Vicolo della Cava
**Galleria d'Arte
Moderna**
Palazzo
Torrigiani
Piazza
S Felice
SERRAGLI
VIA
DE
Calda
**'La Specola'
Museo Zoologico**

8

P
VIA
DE
SERRAGLI
Porta
Romana
Piazzale di
Porta Romana
Giardino
Viale del Cipressi
Font del
Nettuno
**Museo delle
Porcellane**
di Bòboli
**Forte di
Belvedere**
Viale

9

VIALE
NICCOLO
V d Marco
MACHIAVELLI
V d Madonna
V d Pace
V del Bobolino
Istituto
d'Arte
Balano
BOBOLINO
Viale di
S Leon
in An
San

0   250 m
0   250 yds

C   **D**   **E**   **F**

Ponte alle Grazie

Arno

Ch Tedesco
Piazza
d Mozzi
LUNGARNO
Palazzo
Serristori
SERRISTORI
azzo
giani
Museo
Bardini
Via del Renai
Via di
V d G Serristori
San
Niccolò
Via
San
Niccolò
Porta
San Niccolò
Piazza
G Poggi
Via d Fornace
Palazzi
de Mozzi
Via del
Bastioni

SAN NICCOLÒ

Belvedere
di
Viale
Giuseppe
Camping
Michelangelo

Via d Monte alle Croci

David
Piazzale
Michelangelo

VIALE MICHELANGELO

Via di San Miniato al Monte

dell'Erta
Convento d
Stimmatine
San Salvatore
al Monte

Via del Mte alle Croci

Canina

GALILEI

San Míniato
al Monte

Viuzzo d Caprili

GALILEO

Via delle Porte

Passo all'Erta

Cimitero delle
Porte Sante

Erta

Viuzzo di Cartaia

VIALE

Via

G   H   J

STELLA M

Crucifixion before the
Proconsul *(left)* and
The Tribute Money
(right) in the cappella

Part of the thrill of the Cappella Brancacci is observing in Masaccio's frescoes the power of expression and technical brilliance that inspired the Florentine painters of the 15th century.

Minature gem This tiny chapel is reached via the cloisters of the otherwise rather dull Santa Maria del Carmine. Two layers of frescoes commissioned in 1424 by Felice Brancacci, a wealthy Florentine merchant and statesman, illustrate the life of St. Peter, shown in his orange gown. The frescoes were designed by Masolino da Panicale, who began painting them with his brilliant pupil, Masaccio. In 1428 Masaccio took over from Masolino but died that year, aged 27; the rest of the frescoes were completed in the 1480s by Filippino Lippi.

Restoration revelations In the 1980s the chapel was restored, with the removal of accumulated candlesoot and layers of an 18th-century egg-based gum (which had formed a mould). The frescoes now have an intense radiance that makes it possible to see very clearly the shifts in emphasis between Masolino's work and that of Masaccio; contrast the serenity of Masolino's *Temptation of Adam and Eve* with the excruciating agony of Masaccio's *Expulsion of Adam and Eve from Paradise*. The restoration has also highlighted Masaccio's mastery of *chiaroscuro* (light and shade), which, combined with his grasp of perspective, was marvelled at and consciously copied by 15th-century Florentine painters.

THE BASICS

🔢 D6
✉️ Santa Maria del Carmine, Piazza del Carmine (enter through the cloisters)
☎️ 055 238 2195
🕐 Mon, Wed–Sat 10–5, Sun 1–5
🚌 6, D
♿ Poor
💷 Moderate

HIGHLIGHTS

● Masaccio's *Expulsion of Adam and Eve from Paradise*
● Masaccio's *St. Peter heals the Sick*
● Filippino Lippi's *St. Paul visits St. Peter in Prison*
● Masaccio's *Tribute Money*

Giardino di Boboli

Views and fountains abound in the delightful Boboli Gardens, a welcome haven

THE BASICS

✚ E8

✉ Piazza Pitti

☎ 055 265 1838

🕐 Jun–end Aug daily 8.15–7.30; Apr–end May, Sep daily 8.15–6.30; Mar, Oct daily 8.15–5.30; Nov–end Feb daily 8.15–4.30; closed 1st & last Mon of month

🚌 11, 36, 37, D

♿ Good; some areas have steps

💰 Expensive (includes Gardens, Museo delle Porcellane and Museo degli Argenti ▷ 85)

HIGHLIGHTS

● Bacchus fountain (1560)
● La Grotta Grande, a Mannerist cave-cum-sculpture gallery (1583–88)
● Views of the hills from the Giardino dei Cavallieri
● Limonaia (1785)–to protect trees from the frost and now a huge garden shed
● The Isolotto

The Boboli Gardens are, quite literally, a breath of fresh air. They are the only easily accessible reservoir of greenery and tranquillity in Florence, and a lovely retreat after a hard day's sightseeing.

Renaissance origins The Boboli Gardens were created for the Medici when they moved to the Palazzo Pitti in 1550. They represent a superb example of Italian Renaissance gardening, an interplay between nature and artifice expressed in a geometrical arrangement of fountains, grass and low box hedges. In 1766 they were opened to the public, and in 1992 an (unpopular) entrance charge was imposed.

Amphitheatre Just behind the Palazzo Pitti is the amphitheatre, built where the stone for the Palazzo Pitti was quarried. It was the site of the first-ever opera performance and is surrounded by maze-like alleys of fragrant, dusty bay trees. Go uphill past the Neptune Fountain (1565–68) to reach the Giardino dei Cavallieri, where roses and peonies wilt in the summer sun. The pretty building nearby houses the Museo delle Porcellane (Porcelain Museum ▷ 86).

More to see The Viottolone, an avenue of cypresses planted in 1637 and studded with classical statues, leads to the Isolotto, an island set in a murky green pond dotted with pleasantly crumbling statues. In the middle is a copy of Giambologna's *Oceanus* fountain (1576), the original of which is in the Bargello (▷ 24).

Crowds flock up the steps of San Miniato al Monte to view its glorious mosaics

San Miniato al Monte

San Miniato is a wonderful sight on the hill above Florence, its marble façade glistening in the sunlight. Close up it is even more appealing, a jewel of the Romanesque inside and outside.

Christian martyr San Miniato (St. Minias) was an early Christian martyr who came to Florence from the Levant in the 3rd century and was martyred in the Roman amphitheatre that stood on the site of today's Piazza della Signoria, by order of the Emperor Decius. It is said that his decapitated body picked up his head and walked into the hills. His shrine, the site of the present church, was built where he finally collapsed. The church was initially run by Benedictine monks, then by Cluniacs, and finally, from 1373 to the present day, by the Olivetans. In the Benedictine shop on the right as you exit, monks sell honey and herbal potions.

An eagle visitation The church was built in 1018, with a green-and-white marble façade added at the end of the 11th century and mosaics in the 13th century. On the pinnacle a gilded copper statue of an eagle carries a bale of cloth (1410): This is the symbol of the Arte di Calimala, the wool importers' guild, which supported the church in the Middle Ages.

Miraculous crucifix Inside, an inlaid floor (c1207) incorporates zodiac and animal themes. In the nave is a chapel (1448) by Michelozzo, built to house a miraculous crucifix that is now in Santa Trinita.

THE BASICS

⊞ H8

✉ Via Monte alle Croce, off Viale Galileo Galilei

☎ 055 234 2731

🕐 Apr–end Oct daily 8.15–6.30; Nov–end Mar 8–12.30, 2.30–7; closed during services

🚌 12, 13

♿ Poor (make enquires)

🎫 Free

HIGHLIGHTS

- Marble façade
- Inlaid floor
- Mosaics in the apse
- Cappella del Crocifisso
- Wooden ceiling
- Cardinal of Portugal Chapel (1473)

Palazzo Pitti

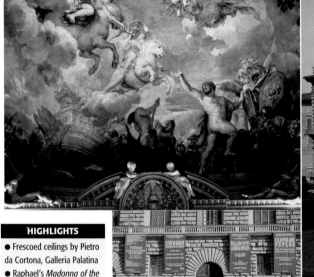

HIGHLIGHTS

● Frescoed ceilings by Pietro da Cortona, Galleria Palatina
● Raphael's *Madonna of the Chair* (c1516)
● Titian's overtly sexual *Mary Magdalene* (c1531)
● Van Dyck's *Charles I and Henrietta Maria* (c1632)
● Titian's *Portrait of a Gentleman* (1540)

TIPS

● It makes sense to concentrate on the Galleria Palatina before moving on to another gallery.
● Be prepared for crowds, and sections to be closed.
● Book ahead to avoid disappointment.
● Leave time to relax afterwards in the Giardino di Boboli (▷ 82). Combined tickets can be bought.

The Pitti Palace, with its four museums, is unremittingly grand, opulent and pompous. Its saving grace is the outstanding collection of Renaissance and baroque art in the Galleria Palatina.

Bigger and better The Palazzo Pitti was built in 1457 to designs by Filippo Brunelleschi for banker Luca Pitti. He wanted it to be bigger and better than the Medici Palace. The result has been likened to a 'rusticated Stalinist ministry'. Ironically, the Medici bought the Palazzo Pitti in 1550 when the Pitti lost their fortune, and it became the residence of the rulers of Florence.

Great art The Galleria Palatina contains baroque and Renaissance works from the Medici collection as important as those in the Uffizi (▷ 30–31).

Cortona's ceiling fresco in the Sala di Marte inside the Palazzo Pitti's Palatine Gallery depicts the Roman God of War (left). The palace houses four museums (below left). The home of the Medici family for three centuries, the imposing Palazzo Pitti was designed in 1458 and enlarged in the 16th century (right)

Highlights include masterpieces by Titian, Raphael and Van Dyck displayed in a haphazard way that reflects the taste of the Medici, who had so many works of art that they didn't worry about hanging them in any order. The Appartamenti Reali (state rooms) are entered through the gallery.

Over the top The Museo degli Argenti (Silver Museum) is a triumph of Medici wealth over taste. Rooms are full of ghoulish reliquaries, Roman glass and Roman and Byzantine vases in *pietra dura* style (inlaid with marble and semi-precious stones) that belong to Lorenzo the Magnificent. Upstairs is a display of cameos, as well as a 17th-century glass Crucifixion scene that is in such appalling taste as to be hilarious. The other two museums are the Galleria del Costume (▷ 86) and the Galleria d'Arte Moderna (▷ 86).

THE BASICS

🚩 E7
✉ Piazza Pitti
☎ Galleria Palatina 055 238 8613; Argenti 055 238 8710
🕐 Galleria Palatina Tue–Sun 8.15–6.50. Argenti daily 8.15–4.30 (7.30 in summer); closed 1st & last Mon of month.
🚌 11, 36, 37, D
♿ Good
🎫 Galleria Palatina, Royal Apartments expensive; Museo degli Argentini (▷ 82)

More to See

FORTE DI BELVEDERE

Built by the Medici in 1590 as a refuge for the Medici Grand Dukes in their struggle against the Florentine Republic, and as a reminder of Medici military might. A lovely place to have a picnic with one of the best views in Florence. Now used for exhibitions.

➕ F8 ✉ Via San Leonardo ☎ 055 277 6406/200 1486 🕐 Grounds only open during exhibitions 🚌 D, C, plus walk 🎫 Free

GALLERIA D'ARTE MODERNA

More than 30 rooms of artwork spanning the mid-18th to mid-20th century. In the main building of the Palazzo Pitti on the floor above the Palatina.

➕ E7 ✉ Palazzo Pitti, Piazza Pitti ☎ 055 238 8616 🕐 Daily 8.15–1.50; closed 2nd and 4th Sun, and 1st, 3rd and 5th Mon of month 🚌 11, 3, 37, D 🚻 Good 🎫 Inclusive ticket with Galleria del Costume moderate

GALLERIA DEL COSTUME

One for devotees to clothes and fashion. The collection illustrates the history of costume from the 18th century up to the 1920s. Displays change frequently, and the gallery hosts many special exhibitions. In the Palazzina Meridiana in the south wing of the Palazzo Pitti.

➕ E7 ✉ Palazzo Pitti, Piazza Pitti ☎ 055 238 8713 🕐 Galleria d'Arte Moderna (➤ above) 🚌 11, 3, 37, D 🚻 Good 🎫 Inclusive ticket with Galleria d'art Moderna moderate

'LA SPECOLA': MUSEO ZOOLOGICO

La Specola is so called after the observatory that used to be here. A highlight is the Cere Anatomiche, a gruesome set of 18th-century wax models of bits of human bodies. Four vignettes of the plague in Florence show rats eating the intestines of decaying bodies. Also hundreds of skeletons and stuffed animals.

➕ E7 ✉ Via Romana 17 ☎ 055 228 8251 🕐 Thu–Tue 9–1; closed hols 🚌 11, 36, D 🚻 Poor 🎫 Moderate

MUSEO DELLE PORCELLANE

French, Italian, German and Viennese porcelain and ceramics in a pavillion at

Museo delle Porcellane

Defensive position–Forte di Belvedere

the top of the Boboli Gardens.
🔒 F8 ✉ Giardino di Boboli, Piazza Pitti
☎ 055 238 8605 ⓘ Boboli Gardens
(▷ 82, panel) 🚌 11, 3, 37, D 🅿 Good,
some steps 🎟 Inclusive ticket with Boboli
Gardens expensive

PIAZZALE MICHELANGELO

Despite the fact that Piazzale
Michelangelo is frequented by bus
loads of tourists, this stupendous vantage point is still very much worth the
trip, either by bus or by foot. Ignore
the poor green copy of Michelangelo's
David and crop of souvenir stalls, be-
ware of pickpockets and soak up the
wonderful view.
🔒 H8 ✉ Viale Galileo Galilei 🚌 12, 13
🅿 Good 🎟 Free

PONTE ALLE GRAZIE

Dating from 1237, when it was known
as Ponte Rubaconte (the bridge over
the River Rubicon), then rebuilt after
World War II to a modern design. Its
name is from the oratory of Santa Maria
delle Grazie, which once stood here.
🔒 G7 🚌 23, C, D

SANTA FELICITÀ

This is the second oldest church in
Florence, dating to the 2nd century AD,
when Syrian and Greek merchants
settled here. The highlight is the
Mannerist *Deposition* (1525–28) by
Pontormo, in the Cappella Caponi, immediately on your right as you enter. It
is a stunning vortex of improbable
forms and hues: lime green, bub-
blegum pink, acid yellow.
🔒 F7 ✉ Piazza Santa Felicità ⓘ Daily
9–12, 3.30–6, Sun 12–1 🍴 D 🅿 Poor
🎟 Free

SANTO SPIRITO

Designed by Filippo Brunelleschi in
1435, with an 18th-century baroque
façade. The *cenacolo* (refectory)
houses 11th-century sculpture and a
beautiful Gothic Crucifixion, believed to
be by the followers of Andrea Orcagna.
🔒 E7 ✉ Piazza Santo Spirito ☎ 055 210
030 ⓘ Sun–Fri 8.30–12, 2–6, Sat 2–6;
closed Wed pm 🍴 D 🅿 Poor 🎟 Free
Refectory ☎ 055 210 030 ⓘ Apr–end
Nov Tue–Sun 9–2; Dec–end Mar 10–1.30;
closed Mon 🅿 Good 🎟 Inexpensive

Get a great view from Piazza Michelangelo

Around Oltrano

Begin amid the bustle of Oltrano, yet you're soon among tranquil surroundings to catch a glimpse of local life and see great views.

DISTANCE: 2km (1 mile) **ALLOW:** 2–3 hours

START

PONTE VECCHIO (▷ 34)
⊞ F7 🚌 B, D

END

PIAZZALE MICHELANGELO (▷ 87)
⊞ H8 🚌 12, 13

❶ In summer this walk can be baking hot; start early in the morning or after 4pm and take a bottle of water. Plan a midday picnic at the Forte di Belvedere (▷ 86).

❷ Set off from the south side of the Ponte Vecchio (▷ 34–35) in Oltrarno. With your back to the bridge, take the first square on your left, Piazza di Santa Felicità.

❸ Here you will find Pontormo's *Deposition* in Santa Felicità (▷ 87) church. Take the road on the left of the church, the Costa di San Giorgio, where Galileo lived at No. 19.

❹ Continue up its steep slope. At the top, you pass through Porta di San Giorgio (1260), the oldest city gate, with a carving of St. George slaying the dragon.

❽ Continue downhill to Piazzale Michelangelo for great views. A No. 12 bus will take you back down to Ponte alle Grazie (▷ 87).

❼ A little way up take the steep Via di San Salvadore al Monte on the left, which crosses Viale Galileo Galilei. Climb the hill flanked by cypress trees that continues up towards San Miniato (▷ 83). Return to Viale Galileo Galilei and go right.

❻ After the entrance to Fort Belvedere, descend steeply along the 13th-century defensive city walls. At the bottom of the hill, by the small gateway of Porta San Miniato, turn right and head up Via del Monte alle Croci.

❺ Follow Via del Belvedere, leaving the 1590 Forte di Belvedere on your right.

WALK

OLTRANO

Shopping

ALCOZER & J
Quirky stylish pieces in a modern idiom using interesting metals and bright stones; costume brooches, necklaces and other items of jewellery.
🔀 E7 ✉ Via Mannelli 15 ☎ 055 623 6346 🚌 D

ANNA
Launched in 1995, this shop is in a 300-year old tower in front of the Pitti Palace. Anna sells a great range of leather goods, bags, knitwear, cashmere, scarves and ties. This is a smart, classic place for both men and women to shop in a quieter part of town.
🔀 E7 ✉ Piazza Pitti 38–40r ☎ 055 283 787 🚌 36, 37, D

ANTICHITÀ CHELINA
Elegant shop with vaulted ceilings and terracotta tile floors, specializing in Italian 15th- and 17th-century paintings, dishes and furniture.
🔀 E7 ✉ Via Maggio 28a ☎ 055 213 471 🚌 11, 36, 37, D

ANTICO SETIFICIO FIORENTINO
Ring the doorbell to gain access to this old Florentine silk factory that provides fabric for some of Italy's most sought-after designers. Much of the fabric is woven using traditional methods and 18th-century looms.
🔀 C6 ✉ Via Lorenzo Bartolini 4 ☎ 055 213 861 🚌 D

BARTOLOZZI & MAIOLI
This antiques shop gives a great insight into the Florentine love of ostentatious adornment. When you wander around you can hear the craftsmen tapping away in the background. Great pieces, but expensive.
🔀 E7 ✉ Via Maggio 13r ☎ 055 239 8633 🚌 11, 36, 37, D

BOTTEGA DEL MOSAICO
The art of the Florentine mosaic, an inlay of hard and semi-precious stones, is unique in the world. The art has been practised for more than 500 years and flourished at

the court of the Medicis. Stones used range from agate to malachite. Examples can be seen in the world's top museums including the Uffizi Gallery (▷ 30–31) in Florence.
🔀 E7 ✉ Via Guicciardini 126r ☎ 055 2210 718 🚌 36, 37, D

BOTTEGA DELLE STAMPE
Framed and unframed antique or art-nouveau prints (known in Italian as Liberty). Elegant.
🔀 E6 ✉ Borgo San Jacopo 56r ☎ 055 295 396 🚌 D

CARNESECCHI
A huge emporium of Italian ceramics, particularly Deruta wares.
🔀 E7 ✉ Via Guicciardini 4r ☎ 055 239 8523 🚌 D

LA CASA DELLA STAMPA
Vivianna is the lithographer who hand-tints many of these beautiful prints. There is a huge selection of Florentine scenes, from the Medici era to the early 19th century, and richly painted studies of butterflies and plants.
🔀 E7 ✉ Sdrucciolo de Pitti 11r ☎ No phone 🚌 11, 36, 37, D

DISS
Charming, unpretentious rustic ceramics, including spotted peasant pots. There is also a selection of glass from Empoli.
🔀 F7 ✉ Via dei Bardi 72r ☎ 055 215 533 🚌 C, D

OLTRANO

SHOPPING

FRANCESCO

For a pair of traditionally handmade shoes or sandals, Francesco may not have the biggest range but it offers quality, value and comfort at low prices.
⊞ E6 ⊠ Via di Santo Spirito 62r ☎ 055 212 428 🚍 11, 36, 37, D

GIOVANNI TURCHI

This huge trove of period pieces is well worth delving into. The store has been in the family for years, and has a huge amount of stock from the local area, Venice and the Veneto. Pieces are less expensive than they would be back home.
⊞ E7 ⊠ Via Maggio 50–52r ☎ 055 217 341 🚍 36, 37, D

GIULIO GIANNINI E FIGLIO

The best-known of Florence's stationery shops, established in 1856, sells tasteful greeting cards and books bound in leather, as well as beautifully finished desk-top paraphernalia, letter racks and pen holders, all covered with marbled paper.
⊞ E7 ⊠ Piazza Pitti 37r ☎ 055 212 621 🚍 36, 37, D

MADOVA GLOVES

A staggering array of fine gloves lined with silk, cashmere and fur in every hue. Family run; established in 1919.
⊞ E7 ⊠ Via Guicciardini 1r ☎ 055 239 6526 🚍 36, 37, D

MARINO

If you are heading south of the river, this is a perfect place for a pastry to set you up for the day. There is a delicious selection of chocolate-, custard- and marmalade-filled *sfogliatelle*, pockets, rounds and tubes and an excellent rum baba.
⊞ D6 ⊠ Piazza Nazarui Sauro ☎ 055 212 657 🚍 11, 36, 37, D

MOLERIA LOCCHI

This shop, next to the Prato dello Strozzino, is reminiscent of a museum, with the most extraordinary examples of glass you will see outside Venice—with prices to match—created using authentic, traditional methods.
⊞ C7 ⊠ Via Domenico Burchiello 10 ☎ 055 229 8371 🚍 C, D

SHOE CITY

The Florentines are famed for making superb shoes. As a testament to the historical importance of the industry in the city's economy, one of the main streets in Florence is named after the shoemakers (Calzaiuoli). The range of shoes available is vast, from the pinnacle of international chic to the value-for-money styles for sale in the market of San Lorenzo. Showrooms at the leather 'factories' in the Santa Croce area are worth a visit.

OLIO & CONVIVIUM

This pristine delicatessen ensures its first-class quality products respect local traditions. Bakery goods, cheeses, charcuterie and other fresh produce are beautifully displayed beside a huge range of olive oils and wine. There's an adjoining restaurant.
⊞ E6 ⊠ Via Santo Spirito 4 ☎ 055 265 8198 🅒 Closed Sun 🚍 6, 11, 36, 37, D

PAOLO PERI

A no-nonsense wine and oil shop selling quality products.
⊞ E7 ⊠ Via Maggio 5r ☎ 055 212 674 🚍 11, 36, D

PITTI CASHMERE

The wisdom and creativity of fine craftsmanship combine to make elegant and beautifully finished cashmere in brilliant and natural hues.
⊞ E7 ⊠ Via dello Sprone 13r ☎ 055 283 516 🚍 11, 36, 37, D

IL TORCHIO

As you walk into this stationery shop you are instantly aware that this is a place where things are made, not just a showroom. You can buy sheets of marbled paper or have it made up to suit your requirements. There are also ready-made marbled paper goods available.
⊞ F7 ⊠ Via dei Bardi 17 ☎ 055 234 2862 🚍 C, D

Entertainment and Nightlife

CABIRIA

A trendy, bohemian bar in Piazza Santo Spirito with outdoor seating. This is Florence's answer to a Left-Bank Paris café. Food is served at all times of the day and night.

➕ E7 ✉ Piazza Santo Spirito 4r ☎ 055 215 732
🕐 Closed Tue 🚌 D

CAFFÈ NOTTE

Pleasantly low-key bar situated close to Piazza Santo Spirito; much frequented by the artists and artisans who live and work in the Oltrarno area. Stays open until 2am.

➕ D7 ✉ Via delle Caldaie 28r ☎ 055 223 067
🕐 Closed Mon 🚌 11, 36, 37, D

CAFFÈ RICCHI

This trendy Oltrano bar is a good place to have coffee during the day, but it

really only comes alive at night, especially in the summer, when you can sit outside.

➕ E7 ✉ Piazza Santo Spirito 9r ☎ 055 215 864
🕐 Closed Sun 🚌 11, 36, 37, D

LA DOLCE VITA

One of the hip places for young Florentines to hang out. A great place for an *aperitivo* and to mingle with the preclub *bella gente*. Open until 2am.

➕ D6 ✉ Piazza del Carmine 6r ☎ 055 284 595 🚌 6, D

HEMINGWAY

Chic, funky café and bar with light meals, great cocktails, specialty teas, fine coffees and chocolates, just off Piazza del Carmine. Stays open until 2am on Friday and Saturday.

➕ D6 ✉ Piazza Piattellina 9r ☎ 055 284 781 🕐 Closed Sun 🚌 6, D

UNIVERSALE

This former cinema space is now dedicated to dance music, cocktail drinking and Italian food. Mid-week focuses on commercial house while Saturday night sees a more eclectic music policy—funk, jazz and exotica.

➕ C6 ✉ Via Pisana 77r ☎ 055 221 122 🕐 Closed Mon, Tue 🚌 6, 12

Restaurants

CAFFÉ PITTI (€–€€)

Just the place for a break in a perfect setting opposite the Palazzo Pitti. You can have breakfast, light lunch, tea or coffee any time. Have a predinner cocktail then a pleasant meal viewing the floodlighted palazzo. Specialty of the house are the hand-picked unique

truffles from the natural reserve owned by the Caffe Pitti, used to create some special dishes.

➕ D6 ✉ Piazza del Carmine 18r ☎ 055 218 601
🕐 Closed Sun 🚌 6, D

CAMMILLO (€€–€€€)

A well-establlished trattoria that attracts an international crowd and a

OLTRANO

ENTERTAINMENT AND NIGHTLIFE/RESTAURANTS

host of Italian celebrities enticed by the excellent home-made pasta, various *baccalà* (salted cod) dishes and expertly cooked meats. Try some of the Masiero family's delicious virgin olive oil with bread. Great choice of Tuscan and Piedmontese wines.

🞣 E6 ✉ Borgo San Jacopo 57r ☎ 055 212 427 🕐 Closed Wed 🚌 11, 36, D

IL CARMINE (€–€€)

Small, friendly trattoria in the delightful Piazza del Carmine. Lengthy (difficult) menu of traditional dishes.

🞣 D6 ✉ Piazza del Carmine 18r ☎ 055 218 601 🕐 Closed Sun 🚌 6, D

LA CASALINGA (€–€€)

This busy family-run establishment is a good place to try *ribollita*, the thick Florentine soup made with bread and vegetables.

🞣 B8 ✉ Via dei Michelozzi 9r ☎ 055 218 624 🕐 Closed Sun 🚌 11, 36, D

MUNACIELLO (€€)

This bistro in the former *scuderie* (stables) of the convent of Santo Spirito serves pizzas as well as excellent Neopolitan fare; the chefs are from the Amalfi coast region. A specialty of the house is *O'Cuoppo*, fried mixed fish in paper with meat and seasonal vegetables. Good choice for an aperitif or cocktail.

🞣 D7 ✉ Via Maffia 31–33r ☎ 055 287 198 🕐 Closed Mon 🚌 11, 36, 37, D

O!O (€–€€)

At this eatery across the river in the district of San Frediano, the fresh approach to Tuscan and Mediterranean organic cooking complements the contemporary design, music and exhibitions.

🞣 D6 ✉ Piazza Piattellina 7r ☎ 055 212 917 🕐 Closed Mon 🚌 6, D

OSTERIO DEL CINGHIALE BIANCO (€€)

The White Boar is named

CONTRADICTION

The concept of vegetarianism is not one that sits easily with Italian ideas about food, and there are very few vegetarian restaurants in Italy. However, there are few better countries for those who do not eat meat (or fish). Many pasta dishes contain no meat–pesto, tomato sauce or ravioli stuffed with spinach and ricotta, to name but a few. For a main course, try *grigliata di verdura* (grilled vegetables) or else restaurant stalwarts such as *parmigiana di melanzane* (aubergine (eggplant) layered with tomato and mozzarella, and baked with a Parmesan crust), *mozzarella in carrozza* (fried mozzarella) and *fritate* (omeletes).

---

after one of Tuscany's greatest culinary specialties. Don't worry there are chicken, veal and rabbit dishes as well.

🞣 E6 ✉ Borgo San Jacopo 43r ☎ 055 215 706 🕐 Closed Wed 🚌 11, 36, D

OSTERIA SANTO SPIRITO (€€)

A delightful trattoria with outdoor seating and a menu of robust main courses and pasta dishes such as penne with lemon and arugula. Lots for vegetarians to munch on and great for kids, too.

🞣 E7 ✉ Piazza Santo Spirito 16r ☎ 055 238 2383 🚌 11, 36, 37, D

AL TRANVAI (€)

Diners are packed into this lively trattoria on the same square as the weekly market. Popular (with locals) is *frattaglie* (a mind-boggling range of offal) but the menu changes every day, with a range of pastas and soups followed by filling vegetable *contorni*.

🞣 C7 ✉ Piazza Torquato Tasso 14 ☎ 055 225 197 🕐 Closed Sat lunch, Sun 🚌 12, 13

LE VOLPI E L'UVA (€€)

A good little wine bar behind the Ponte Vecchio where you can wash down pungent Italian salamis and cheeses with robust Tuscan wines.

🞣 F7 ✉ Piazza dei Rossi ☎ 055 239 8132 🕐 Closed Sun 🚌 C, D

There is plenty to do to escape the crowds or to have a change of scenery. Chose from pretty Fiesole, only 7km (4 miles) away; try medieval Siena and Lucca; or the Leaning Tower of Pisa, providing an irresistible pull.

Knight in shining armour (left) and delicate paintings (below) at the Museo Stibbert

Museo Stibbert

This wonderfully bizarre museum, with one of the finest collections of armour in the world is a welcome break from the more serious musems of Florence; and offers a chance to picnic in the grounds of a huge surburban villa.

Eccentric collection Born to an English father and Italian mother Frederick Stibbert (1838–1906) inherited an enormous amount of money and indulged much of it in his great passions for travel and collecting. He extended the 14th-century house and turned a section of the vast result into a museum to house his booty. When he died, he left the house and its contents to the British government who passed it on to the city.

World-class armour What is on display in the museum is only a part of the total collection. The once decaying house and grounds are being continually restored. The style is heavily decorative; particularly the Sala da Ballo (ballroom), a completely over-the-top confection of Empire Style in red and gold. Some 64 rooms display an extraordinary array of objects from porcelain and shoe buckles to armour and weapons. Don't miss the Sala della Cavalcata with fully armed 16th-century knights on horseback, the Sala del Condottiere, complete with large equestrian figure and the fine collection of Islamic armour and costume.

Take a break The wooded grounds of the museum, complete with Egyptian-style folly, present a shady retreat from the heat and crowds of the city.

THE BASICS

➕ Off map at F1
✉ Via Federico Stibbert 26
☎ 055 475 520/055 486 049
🕐 Mon–Wed 10–2, Fri–Sun 10–6; ticket office closes 1 hour before museum
🚌 4 to Via Vittorio Emanuele II and steep 5-minute walk to museum.
♿ Most parts have access
🎫 Moderate

HIGHLIGHTS

● Sala della Cavalcata
● Sala del Condottiere
● Sala da Ballo
● Islamic armour collection
● Victorian-landscaped grounds

FARTHER AFIELD

★

TOP 25

97

More to See

LE CASCINE

Florence's largest park is a long way from the heart of town, badly kept and seedy by night. Long and thin, it was laid out as a public park by Napoleon's sister Elisa Baciocchi Bonaparte in 1811, on the site of the Medici dairy pastures (*cascine*). Every Tuesday there is a market, and an open-air swimming pool is also in the park.

➕ A3 ✉ Ponte della Vittoria 🕐 24 hours 🚌 17 ♿ Good 🎫 Free

CERTOSA DI GALLUZZO

This great Carthusian monastery was once occupied by 18 monks, who lived silent lives. The stunning Chiostro Grande is decorated with *tondi* by brothers Andrea and Giovanni della Robbia. The visit includes the Palazzo degli Studi, which holds great *Scenes from the Passion* frescoes, executed by Pontormo while he was sheltered here during the 1522 plague.

➕ Off map at C9 ✉ Certosa di Galluzzo, Via Buca di Certose 🕐 055 204 9226 🕐 Tue–Sun 9.15–11.30, 3–4.30 🚌 37 ♿ Good 🎫 Free or donation ❓ Guided tours only

FIESOLE

Perched on a hillside 7km (4 miles) above Florence, this delightful place was originally an Etruscan settlement, that grew in importance under the Romans. Evidence of this can be seen in the Area Archeologica, as well as the Roman amphitheatre, baths and temple, and the impressive Etruscan remains. The cathedral, shops and restaurants are on Piazza Mino da Fiesole. From here walk up Via di San Francesco for wonderful views.

➕ Off map at M1 ℹ Via Portigiani 3–5 (🕐 055 598 720 🕐 Mar–end Oct Mon–Sat 9–6, Sun 10–1, 2–6; Nov–end Feb Mon–Sat 9–5, Sun 10–4 🚌 7 (buses depart from Santa Maria Novella station or San Marco)

FORTEZZA DA BASSO

An enormous defensive fortress built in 1534 by Antonio da Sangallo il Giovane to the orders of Alessandro de' Medici. Today cars and buses hurtle around all sides, while the citadel plays host to events and exhibitions.

➕ E3 ✉ Viale Filippo Strozzi 🕐 055 36931 🚌 4, 12, 13, 14, 20, 23, 28, 33, 80

Roman ampitheatre, part of the Museo Fiesole

Excursions

LUCCA

A prosperous town entirely enclosed within superb Renaissance walls with a rich heritage of churches and palaces.

The best starting point is Piazza Napoleone, with all the main sights only a few minutes' walk away. Begin at the Duomo, and its Museo della Cattedrale, then cross the square to Santi Giovanni e Reparata. Via Fillungo is an expensive shopping street that leads north to the Piazza Anfiteatro and San Frediano, another outstanding church. The main museums lie inside the walls to the west and east of the heart of town. Walking around the walls gives a fine overview of the town.

THE BASICS

Lucca
Distance: 50km (31 miles)
Journey Time about 1 hour
🚆 Regular departures from Santa Maria Novella station to Lucca Centrale
ℹ Piazza Maria 35
☎ 0583 919 931

PISA

The main draw is the stunning architecture of the Campo dei Miracoli (Field of Miracles), home to the famous Leaning Tower.

The tower, reopened in 2001 after years of work to steady the tilt, stands next to the Romanesque-Gothic Duomo and Baptistery, the largest in Italy. All three buildings date from the 11th and 12th centuries, at the height of Pisa's power.

THE BASICS

Pisa
Distance: 80km (50 miles)
Journey Time 1 hour
🚆 Regular departures from Santa Maria Novella station to Pisa Centrale Station
ℹ Piazza del Duomo
☎ 050 560 464

FARTHER AFIELD

EXCURSIONS

Don't miss the Leaning Tower of Pisa
Flower market in Lucca

SIENA

One of the loveliest towns in Italy, with great museums, interesting shops and many hills.

The focal point is fan-shaped Piazza del Campo, which slopes down to the bell tower. The Gothic cathedral was built between 1136 and 1382. Outside is a vast unfinished nave, begun in 1339 with the intention of making this the world's largest cathedral. Work was abandoned during the plague of 1348. Siena is home to the famous Palio, a horse race held in Piazza del Campo on 2 July and 16 August.

TUSCAN COUNTRYSIDE

A country drive is a real treat. Much-visited San Gimignano is a prime destination with its hilltop site and medieval towers.

For pots, stop in Montelupo, where many of Florence's ceramics have been made for centuries. On your way back visit Vinci, the birthplace of Leonardo da Vinci with a museum about his life. If you want a swim, the village of Sambuca, near Tavarnelle, has an outdoor pool. Deep in the countryside you can find olives and wine for sale.

The vast Piazza del Campo, Siena

Shopping

Lucca

LA CACIOTECA

A tiny food shop selling a host of local and traditional seasonal produce. Staff are friendly and even if your command of Italian is weak they always try and help.

✉ Via Fillungo ☎ 0583 496 346 🕐 Mon–Sat 7–8, plus every 3rd Sun of month

CARIOLOA

On Lucca's main square, this is one of the best of the many ceramics shops in town. Goods are not mass produced and relatively reasonably priced, with a wide range of designs, both traditional and modern.

✉ Piazza San Michele 10 ☎ 0583 467 677 🕐 Mon–Sat 7–8, plus every 3rd Sun of month

CERAMISTI D'ART

The Tuscan artists Stefano Seardo and Fabrizio Falchi sculpt and paint at this workshop. Visit to pick up hand-painted decorative tiles, terracotta sculptures and marble mosaics. Everything is produced according to ancient Italian ceramic techniques.

✉ Via Mordini 74/78 ☎ 0583 491 119 🕐 Tue–Sun 9.30–1, 3.30–7.30, Mon 3.30–7.30

MARSILI COSTANTINO

Marsali gives a tasty introduction to Lucca's local vineyards, with some lesser-known but delicious wines. Also try some of the herb liqueurs and *digestifs* that are produced using local recipes.

✉ Piazza San Michele 38 ☎ 0583 491 751 🕐 Jun–end Sep daily 9–7.30; Oct–end May Tue–Sat 9–1, 3.30–7.30, Mon 3.30–7.30

Pisa

FEDERICO SALZA

This Pisan outlet of popular Turin confectioner sells beautiful fashioned chocolates and pastry goods. Look for the chocolate Leaning Tower of Pisa.

✉ Borgo Stretto 46 ☎ 050 580 244 🕐 Jun–end Oct daily 8–8.30; Nov–end May Tue–Sun 8–8.30

LENZI GHINO GIACOMO

This factory shop, to the west of Pisa towards Vicopisano, sells classic Tuscan ceramics and

HANDICRAFTS

Tuscany has a strong artisan tradition that continues to flourish. There is a huge range of regional handicrafts to seek out, such as olive-wood bowls and plates, alabaster ware and glassware, with many products only available in the area where they are made. Florence and the surrounding area has an abundance of small craft workshops specializing in picture frames, accessories and restored antique furniture.

pride themselves on producing basins, vases and pottery the traditional way. Choose from vases and crockery splashed with green and white—they are beautifully decorated pots for storing oil, wine and herbs and make great gifts.

✉ Via Provinciale Vicarese 371, San Giovanni alla Vena ☎ 050 799 015 🕐 Mon–Sat 9–1, 3–8

PAOLO CAPRI

Designer Paolo Capri's showroom is a popular outlet for jewellery, watches and frames, where most of the items are created by Florentine silversmiths. There is also a range of giftware that takes its inspiration from local traditions and culture.

✉ Via di Marino 2 ☎ 050 577 111 🕐 Tue–Sat 9–1, 4–7, Mon 4–7

I PASANI

This delicatessen (7km/4 miles north of Pisa on the Brennero road towards Lucca) sells a selection of the tastiest food, produced by the best local artisans. Shop for truffles, extra virgin olive oils, cheeses, salami, sauces and much more. The English-speaking staff can provide recommended recipes as well as all the cooking adice you might require.

✉ Via di Signano 25A, San Giuliano Terme ☎ 050 816 025 🕐 Mon–Fri 9–1, 2–6

Siena

ANTICHITÀ MONNA ANGESE

One of Siena's better antiques stores, stocking furniture and silver amid other items. There is another, smaller shop on the opposite side of the street, which deals in antique jewellery.
✉ Via di Città 45 ☎ 0577 280 205

CERMICHE ARTISHICHE SANTA CATERINA

A family business run by the founder, Marcello Neri, his wife and son. The whole family works in the traditional Sienese styles of ceramics using only black, white and *terra di Siena,* or burnt siena glass glazes. Their designs are inspired by local architecture, especially the Duomo, and you can watch them at work.
✉ Via di Città 74 ☎ 0577 283 098

CORTECCI ABBIGLIAMENTO

A large collection of men's and women's designer labels including Gucci, Armani, Yves Saint Laurent, Christian Dior, Roberto Cavalli and Dolce & Gabbana. There are two branches of this shop and this one has the more classic collections, while the other branch at Il Campo 30, stocks labels aimed at a younger market.

✉ Via Banchi di Sopra 27 ☎ 0577 280 096

DROGHERIA MANGANELLI

A must for foodies. It is a member of the Slow Food Movement, an organization that promotes organic food, grown and cooked using traditional method. Drogheria Manganelli has been selling local produce since 1879, including cured meats, fine farmhouse cheeses, vinegars, wine, the best of virgin olive oil, *ricciarelli* (almond cookies) traditionally served with sweet wine) are enjoyed year round.
✉ Via delle Campane 9 ☎ 0577 282 290

MARKETS

There are daily food markets in provincial and regional capitals and other large towns. They generally take place in a purpose-built market hall or in a specific square or street, selling meat, groceries, fish, dairy products, fruit and vegetables. Where there's a daily food market, the weekly market will be devoted to everything else from clothes and shoes to household goods, plants and fabrics. In Florence the most prominent are Mercato Centrale (▷ 68), Mercato di Sant'Ambrogio and Mercato Nuovo (▷ 38).

MORBIDI

One of the best-known Sienese delicatessens, selling Tuscan salamis and the more unusual *finochiona* (salami made from fennel). Be sure to try the local cheeses, such as *pecorino* or the oval-shaped *fresco di Monnalisa*, and pâtés that are great for picnics.
✉ Via Banchi di Sopra 75 ☎ 0577 280 268

SIENA RICAMA

This embroidery and needlework shop is run by Signora Fontani, who makes all the goods himself. Drawing inspiration from medieval designs, local art, frescoes and manuscripts, the embroidered or cross-stitched items include clothing, soft furnishings, lampshades and tapestries.
✉ Via di Città 61 ☎ 0577 288 339

TESSUTI A MANO

Drop into this workshop and boutique to pick up beautiful, hand-woven accessories and fashionable garments. Designer Fioretta Bacci can often be seen sitting at a loom weaving her much sought-after scarves, shawls and items of clothing.
✉ Via San Pietro 7 ☎ 0577 282 200

Entertainment and Nightlife

AUDITORIUM FLOG

This is probably the best known of Florence's live music venues, where music of all kinds is performed; regular themed disco evenings.
🔳 Off map 🖂 Via Mercati 24b ☎ 055 487 145; box office 055 210 804 🚍 4

CENTRAL PARK

This is a true house-music complex, complete with garden, eight bars, four dance floors, restaurant and VIP terrace. Italian house dominates but there's also plenty of room for loungecore and smooth piano-bar music.
🔳 B4 🖂 Via del Fosso Macinate 2 ☎ 055 353 505 🕐 Closed Mon 🚍 1, 9, 12, 80

ESTATE FIESOLANA

A season of music, opera and ballet known as the Sunset Concerts, primarily in the open-air Teatro Romano in Fiesole (▷ 98), from late June to September. Reserve in advance and then head for the verdant and tranquil Fiesole hills, above the city. The concerts are an unbeatable experience.
Estate Fiesolana
🔳 Off map 🖂 Via Partigiana, Fiesole (ticket office for Roman theatre) ☎ 055 59187; www.estatefiesolana.com
Roman Theatre
🔳 Off map 🖂 Via Marini 🚍 7
General Box Office
🔳 Off map 🖂 Via Alamanni 39 ☎ 055 210 804

GIRASOL

Florentines have a passion for Latin American bars. This is the best, with live and recorded Cuban, Caribbean and other Latin-American music.
🔳 D1 🖂 Via del Romito 1r ☎ 055 474 948 🚍 14

PALASPORT

This medium-size venue near Campo Marte hosts some of Italy's most celebrated rock and pop acts like Pino Daniele and Ligabue. Check in advance for well-known British and US bands who maybe swinging into Palasport.
🔳 M4 🖂 Viale P Paoli 3 ☎ 055 678 841 🚍 3, 10

PALAZZO DEI CONGRESSI

This palazzo hosts many conferences and cultural events throughout the year. Look out for the occasional choral and classical concerts held in

MAGGIO MUSICALE

This major musical festival held between May and early July includes opera and ballet as well as orchestral concerts and chamber music. It has its own orchestra, chorus and ballet troupe. The main venue is the Teatro Comunale; the Teatro della Pergola and the Teatro Verdi are used for more intimate recitals. The main box office is the Teatro Comunale.

one of the fine salons.
🔳 E3 🖂 Viale Filippo Strozzi ☎ 055 497 21 🚍 6, 11, 22, 36, 37, A

PINOCCHIO JAZZ

Some of Italy's top jazz artists can be heard during the club's two-season agenda. Members nod approvingly in this smoky venue while the enthusiastic musicians play their instruments into the night. Check *Firenze Spettacolo* for what's on.
🔳 M8 🖂 Viale Giannotti 13 ☎ 055 683 388 🚍 31, 32

MECCANO

This large and popular hip club caters for a wide range of tastes including mainstream, house and funk, primarily aimed at a young crowd. It's like one big house party on several floors and a chance to let your hair down after all that culture.
🔳 B4 🖂 Via degli Olmi, Parco delle Cascine ☎ 055 331 371 🕐 Closed Mon, Sun 🚍 1, 9, 27,80

TENAX

Trendy and up-to-date music and a huge dance floor; very popular with both Florentines and foreigners. As a superclub, it has some mind-blowing lighting and sound technology and some very curious art installations. Also hosts various live music acts.
🔳 Off map 🖂 Via Pratese 46 ☎ 055 308 160 🕐 Closed Mon 🚍 29, 30

Sport

CENTRO SPORTIVO DLF

Indoor and outdoor courts for tennis can be found in Le Cascine's sports complex.

➕ B3 ✉ Via Paisiello 131, Le Cascine ☎ 055 363 052 🚌 1, 9, 12, 16, 26, 27, 80

CIRCOLO DI TENNIS

Florence's oldest tennis club, established in 1898, has 10 clay courts.

➕ B4 ✉ Viale del Visarno 1, Le Cascine ☎ 055 354 326 🚌 1, 9, 12, 16, 26, 27, 80

GOLF CLUB MONTELUPO

This 3,067 yard, par 36, 9-hole golf course lies below the Chianti Montalbano hills on the banks of the Arno. Enjoy the wonderful scenery and the excellent facilities that include a pro shop, practice area and putting greens. Coaching available.

➕ Off map ✉ Fattoria di Fibbiana, Via le Piagge 4, Montelupo (19 km/12 miles to west of Florence) ☎ 0571 541 004

ICE SKATING IN THE CITY

In December and January each year, a temporary ice rink is constructed in the Fortezza da Basso or Piazza Santa Croce (▷ 27). As you glide around you can admire the imposting military structure of the fortress. The architecture of the palaces in Santa Croce is also wonderful.

➕ E3 ✉ Fortezza de Basso 🚌 4, 12, 13, 20, 23, 28, 33, 80

IPPODROME DELLE MULINA

The Ippodromo delle Mulina is the place to go and see horseracing in Florence where you will find flat racing or chariot racing. Phone or check the local press for meetings. Also stages polo events.

➕ B4 ✉ Le Cascine ☎ 055 411 107 🚌 14

PAGANELLI

This renovated swimming pool to the northwest of the city, is worth visiting at any time of the year. As well as being open six days a week for swimming, there are courses

for adults and children, including diving and aquagym.

➕ Off map ✉ Viale Guidoni 208, Novoli ☎ 055 437 9787 🕐 Closed Tue 🚌 5, 22

PALESTRA TROPOS

This well-established gym has lots of classes for all ages including aerobics and hydrobike exercises.

➕ K6 ✉ Via Orcagna 20a ☎ 055 679 746 🚌 14, 31, 32

PISCINA COMUNALE BELLARIVA

An outdoor Olympic swimming pool with a smaller one for children in pleasant shady gardens east of the city.

➕ M7 ✉ Lungarno A Moro ☎ 055 677 521 🕐 Jun–Sep 🚌 14

PISCINA LE PAVONIERE

Most popular and prettiest outdoor swimming pool in Florence, in Le Cascine (▷ 98).

➕ A4 ✉ Viale della Catena 2 ☎ 055 321 5644 🕐 Jun–Sep 🚌 17

STADIO COMUNAL ARTEMIO FRANCHI

The magnificent Stadio Comunale Artemio Franchi or the Palazzo dello Sport, is where AC Fiorentina (▷ panel) play football (soccer). Games take place on alternate Sundays from September to May.

➕ L3 ✉ Campo di Marte, Viale Manfredo Fanti 4 ☎ 055 587 858 🚌 17

Restaurants

PRICES

Prices are approximate, based on a 3-course meal for one person.

€€€ over €45
€€ €20–€45
€ under €20

Fiesole

RISTORANTE I POLPA (€€)

Eat at this friendly place and enjoy a magnificent night-view over Florence. Not only is there an open wood-burning grill, but the oven is lighted too, for cooking *crostini*—toasted crusty bread with a variety of toppings that make tasty starters.

⊞ Off map at M1 ⊠ Piazza Mino da Fiesole 21–22 ☎ 055 50485 🕔 Thu–Tue 7–10 🚍 7

RISTORANTE PERSEUS (€€)

This is one of Florence's best restaurants in which to sample the famous *bistecca alla fiorentina* (▷ panel). Other classic Tuscan dishes are served on a terrace facing the Teatro Romano in Fiesole.

⊞ Off map at M1 ⊠ Piazza Mino da Fiesole 9 ☎ 055 591 43 🕔 Limited winter opening 🚍 7

RISTORANTE SAN MICHELE (€€€)

It's evocative former monastery setting and some of the finest cuisine in the area attract diners to this Fiesole restaurant

in the hotel Villa San Michele (▷ 112).

⊞ Off map at M1 ⊠ Via Doccia 4 ☎ 055 567 8200 🕔 Daily lunch and dinner; closed end-Nov to end-Mar 🚍 7

Lucca

BARSOTTI DA GUIDO (€–€€)

Small trattoria a few paces from Piazza San Salvatore in the middle of Lucca. Predominantly Tuscan and Lucchese cusine with the usual mixture of cold cuts, a range of interesting sausages, grilled meats, roasts and home-made pastas. There is no English menu but staff are happy to translate. Small but well-chosen wine list to complement your meal.

NATURALLY ROBUST

The classic Florentine dish is *bistecca alla fiorentina* (T-bone steak sold by the weight, usually 100g). Grilled and served rare with lemon, it can be found in the majority of Florentine restaurants. Other traditional dishes include *trippa alla fiorentina* (tripe stewed with tomatoes and served with Parmesan), *crostini* (toasted bread and a pâté of roughly chopped chicken livers), and *panzanella* (a salad of crumbled bread tossed with tomatoes with olive oil, onions, basil and parsley).

⊠ Via C Battisti 28 ☎ 0583 467 219 🕔 Mon–Sat lunch and dinner

BUCA DI SAN ANTONIO (€€)

One of the oldest, as well as the most popular, restaurants in Lucca. The menu is all à la carte, with an emphasis on Lucchese cuisine, and the use of seasonal, freshly-produced ingredients.

⊠ Via della Cervia 3 ☎ 0583 55881 🕔 Tue–Sat lunch and dinner, Sun lunch only

DANTE (€€)

Small, relatively quiet restaurant serving dishes typical of the Lucca area, including home-made ravioli stuffed with wild mushrooms and grilled meats. The à la carte menu also has wine recommendations to accompany your selection.

⊠ Via delle Gavine 72 ☎ 0584 956 046 🕔 Closed Mon, Wed

TRATTORIA DA LEO (€)

Popular family-run trattoria where you can eat in the dining room, with its pastel walls and wooden furnishings, or on the simple but shaded terrace. The owners make you feel at home, sometimes pulling up a chair and chatting after the meal.

⊠ Via Tegrimi 1 ☎ 0583 492 236 🕔 Daily lunch and dinner

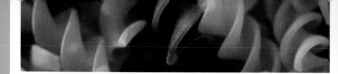

Pisa

DE BRUNO (€€)

Self-proclaimed as the best restaurant in Pisa, this long-established trattoria serves traditional local cuisine. The two dining rooms have wood-beamed ceilings, long, elegant tables, and white-washed walls covered with photographs of the famous people who have dined here under patron Piero Cei's watchful eye. Reserve in advance.

✉ Via Luigi Bianchi 12
☎ 050 560 818 🕐 Wed–Sun lunch and dinner, Mon lunch only

LA BUCA (€–€€)

In a popular spot in the heart of Pisa, Buca draws the crowds to its pleasant terrace and the set-price lunch menu, which offers Tuscan cuisine at a reasonable price. Dinner is little more formal but still with lots of pizza and pasta choices.

✉ Via G Tassi 6/B ☎ 050 560 660 🕐 Sun–Thu lunch and dinner

Siena

AL MANGIA (€€€)

In a great spot overlooking the Piazza del Campo. Run by a a fourth generation of the Senni family, the restaurant is tastefully decorated and serves typical local meat and fish dishes.

✉ Piazza del Campo 42–46
☎ 0577 281 121 🕐 Lunch and dinner; closed Wed, Nov–Mar

IL BIONDO (€€–€€€)

Down a quiet side street lined with medieval buildings. In summer try to reserve a table on the terrace overlooking the piazza. This place is worth splurging out on if you enjoy good food.

✉ Via del Rustichetto Angolo Piazza Posta ☎ 0577 280 739 🕐 Thu–Tue lunch and dinner

IL CAMPO (€–€€)

This is the original restaurant on the Piazza del Campo and a great spot for people-watching. A consequence of this is that service may suffer at busy times. The menu is a mix of Italian and European cusine. No reservations.

ICE CREAM

Italian ice cream–*gelato*–is generally of very high quality. Italians would rather pay more and eat something made with fresh ingredients. So a basic ice cream is usually made with milk, cream, eggs and sugar, and the tastes are strikingly pure and direct. A popular choice is *crema*–egg custard–good with a scoop of intense dark chocolate or pungent coffee. People usually opt for a selection of *creme* or *frutte* (creams or fruit) and don't mix the two types. The best *gelaterie* serve fruit varieties made from whatever fruits are in season.

✉ Piazza del Campo 50–51
☎ 0577 280 725
🕐 Wed–Mon lunch and dinner

OSTERIA LE LOGGE (€€–€€€)

In a former medieval pharmacy, this charming restaurant is just off the Campo. There are tables outside, plus two dining areas. The menu is full of simple, classic Tuscan dishes. Reservations advised.

✉ Via del Porrione 33
☎ 0577 48013 🕐 Mon–Sat lunch and dinner

SOTTO LE FONTI (€€)

This medieval building has been renovated to re-create an old-fashioned restaurant. The menu is based on Sienese dishes, such as salami, game, or lamb chops with juniper. The scrumptious cakes and desserts are all home-made.

✉ Via Esterna Fonteblanda 14 ☎ 0577 226 226

LA TAVERNA DI SAN GIUSEPPE (€–€€)

A lively group of young people run this trattoria. It specializes in Tuscan food, with an emphasis on meat, although vegetarians are well catered for with a rich vegetable soup, *ribollita*. Initimate cellar-like dining room.

✉ Via Giovanni Duprè 132
☎ 0577 42286 🕐 Mon–Sat lunch and dinner; closed last 2 weeks in Jan and Jul

Florence is one of Italy's top destinations and hotels are, on the whole, expensive. Check out the Internet before leaving home to catch some seasonal deals. Staying out of season is your best bet.

Where to Stay

Introduction

Choose from world-class hotels in historic buildings, ultra chic boutique hotels or family-run pensiones that haven't changed much in 30 years. Houses and apartments offering bed and breakfast is an option becoming very popular.

Hotels
Tuscan hotels (*alberghi*) are graded by the regional authorities on a star rating of one to five. These refer to the facilities provided rather than character or comfort. Expect five-star hotels to be grand, with superb facilities and service; four-star establishments will be almost as good. Three-star hotels are more idiosyncratic. Prices can vary enormously, as can the public areas and staffing levels; but all rooms will have a television and telephone. One and two stars are relatively inexpensive, clean and comfortable, and rooms almost always have private bathrooms in two-star places. Breakfast is usually included, although often poor.

Pensiones
There's little difference between simpler hotels and *pensiones*; both are usually family-run, and provide spotlessly clean, comfortable rooms at a fair price. Some *pensiones* may be a bit dated, but this is also the case in smaller hotels.

Rooms to Rent
Signs saying rooms (*carnere* or *zimmer*) are rooms to rent in private houses and are a good option if money is tight or you can't find a hotel. Local tourist offices keep a list.

RESERVATIONS

Florence is so popular that you will need to book in advance at whatever time of year you decide to visit. If you're booking in advance from home, make certain you get written confirmation and take it with you. Without this, you may turn up and find all knowledge of your booking denied. If you make an internet booking, be sure to print out your book confirmation and take it with you.

You will appreciate somewhere comfortable to relax and unwind after your journey or a day sightseeing

Budget Hotels

WHERE TO STAY BUDGET HOTELS

PRICES

Expect to pay up to €100 for a budget hotel for a double room

BRETAGNA

Eighteen affordable rooms with views of the River Arno.

➕ E6 ✉ Lungarno Corsini 6 ☎ 055 289 618; fax 055 289 619 🚌 B

CHIAZZA

www.hotelchiazza.com
In the Santa Croce area, this hotel has been refurbished and offers a smart, comfortable budget option. Not far from the Duomo, some of the 14 rooms look out onto the terracotta-tiled rooftops.

➕ H5 ✉ Borgo Piniti 5 ☎ 055 248 0363; fax 055 234 6888 🚌 14, 23

CRISTINA

A small, friendly hotel in a medieval palace off a quiet street in the heart of Florence. The nine rooms (four en-suite) have high ceilings and wood furniture. Good value and the delightful owners make it perfect for families. Because of this it is a popular choice so make reservations well ahead.

➕ F6 ✉ Via della Condotta 4 ☎ 055 214 484 🚌 A

FIRENZE

A 57-room modern hotel in a very quiet courtyard in the heart of Florence.

➕ F6 ✉ Piazza dei Donati 4 ☎ 055 214 203; fax 055 212 370 🚌 A

JOHANNA I

www.johanna.it
The owners have created a homey, laid-back feel. The 11 rooms are small but beautifully furnished and there is a cozy communal room with a fridge.

➕ G3 ✉ Via Bonifacio Lupi 14 ☎ 055 481 896; fax: 055 482 721 🚌 4, 12, 20, 33

PENSIONE MARIA LUISA DE' MEDICI

Characterful 17th-century house cluttered with objects d'art. The nine rooms vary in size—some very large and two with private bathroom. Excellent value with breakfast included, and very close to the Duomo. Not for night owls as the owner has an 11 o'clock curfew.

➕ F5 ✉ Via del Corso 1 ☎ 055 280 048 🚌 14, 23, A

CAMPING

Campeggio Michelangelo is on the hills south of the Arno yet is only a short bus ride to central Florence. It has hot showers, clean toilets, washing machines, electricity points, Internet access, a supermarket and a bar with a terrace that looks out over the city. There are 95 pitches.
Open all year

➕ H8 ✉ Via Michelangelo 80 ☎ 055 681 1977; www.camping.it 🚌 12, 13

NUOVA ITALIA

www.nuovaitalia.hotelinfirenze.it
Modern, clean 20-room hotel with friendly staff.

➕ E4 ✉ Via Faenza 26 ☎ 055 268 430; fax 055 210 941 🚌 4, 12

SORELLE BANDINI

Perfect for the more bohemian traveller, this *pensione* is on the top floor of a 1505 palazzo and has a fabulous loggia ideal for picnics, and 12 huge rooms (one with bathroom) with frescoed, slightly crumbling ceilings. The breakfast room looks over a panorama of terracotta tile roofs to the Palazzo Pitti.

➕ E7 ✉ Piazza Santo Spirito 9 ☎ 055 215 308; fax 055 282 761 🚌 D

SCOTI

www.hotelscoti.com
Atmospheric 15th-century building in an excellent location directly opposite the Palazzo Strozzi in the shopping mecca of Via de' Tornabuoni. It's a great place to stay—excellent value, with period character, and a good central base from which to explore the city. The 11 bedrooms are simple and light. There are no private bathrooms, but the shared ones are very clean. The lounge area has attractive 18th-century frescoes depicting Italian landscapes.

➕ E6 ✉ Via de' Tornabuoni 7 ☎ Tel/fax 055 292 128 🚌 6, 11, 36, A

Mid-Range Hotels

PRICES

Expect to pay between €100 and €200 for a double room in a mid-range hotel

ALESSANDRA

www.hotelalessandra.com
Two-star hotel in a small street that runs parallel to the Arno. The 27 guest rooms are spacious, clean and neat, but not all have a private bathroom.
🔼 F6 ✉ Borgo S.S. Apostoli 17 ☎ 055 283 438; fax 055 210 619 🚌 6, 11, 36, 37

ANNALENA

www.hotelannalena.it
In a Medici palazzo opposite the Boboli Gardens, this hotel was once the haunt of artists and writers. Some of the 20 rooms have terraces and views. A lovely peaceful spot.
🔼 D8 ✉ Via Romana 34 ☎ 055 222 402; fax 055 222 403 🚌 11, 36, 37, D

BALESTRI

www.hotel-balestri.it
Close to the River Arno, between the Uffizi and Santa Croce, with 46 comfortable rooms.
🔼 F5 ✉ Piazza Mentana 7 ☎ 055 214 743; fax 055 239 8042 🚌 B

BELLETTINI

www.hotelbellettini.com
Close to San Lorenzo and the Duomo, this hotel, with 28 rooms and 5 suites, dates from the 15th century, making it one of the oldest in Florence as well as one of the friendliest. Rooms come in a variety of sizes; optional private bathroom. Breakfast includes owner's home baking and should not be missed.
🔼 F5 ✉ Via de'Conti 7 ☎ 055 213 561; fax 055 283 551 🚌 1, 6, 7, 10, 11, 14, 17, 23

CASCI

www.hotelcasci.com
A family-run hotel, with 25 rooms, and once home to the Italian composer Gioacchino Rossini. Although modernized, it still has some of its original 14th-century features. Immaculate functional rooms a short stroll from the Duomo.
🔼 F4 ✉ Via Cavour 13 ☎ 055 211 686; fax 033 239 6461 🚌 1, 6, 7, 10, 17, 31, 32

LE DUE FONTANE

Modern 57-room hotel in the delightful Piazza della

WHICH ROOM?

The room with a view is a much sought-after thing. However, it can often come with street noise. Most Florentine rooms are in palazzi built around courtyards, so the rooms with views face onto the street, while the ones looking over the courtyards are pleasantly quiet. You might like to forego the romance to ensure a good night's sleep.

Santissima Annunziata.
🔼 G4 ✉ Piazza della Santissima Annunziata 14 ☎ 055 210 185; fax 055 294 461 🚌 6, 31, 32, C

GALILEO

www.galileohotel.it
Bright and cheerful hotel ideal for those who want to make the most of every minute in Florence. The 31 rooms are clean and relaxing and have the amenities you might require.
🔼 E4 ✉ Via Nazionale 22a ☎ 055 496 645; fax 055 469 447 🚌 4, 12, 25, 31, 32

LOGGIATO DEI SERVITI

www.loggiatodeiservitihotel.it
You can relax under vaulted ceilings, amid dark-wood antiques and rich fabrics in the former monastery of the Serviti. The refurbished rooms are enlivened by bright curtains and throws. Many look onto the arcades of Piazza Santissima Annunziate. The 29 rooms have private bathrooms and the breakfast room has views of the Accademia gardens.
🔼 G4 ✉ Piazza Santissima Annunziata 3 ☎ 055 239 9544; fax 055 260 8908 🚌 11, 36, 37, D

MARIO'S

www.hotemarios.com
This small family-run hotel is an example of the great value for money that can still be found in this expensive city. It feels as if you are staying in

someone's home, with care and attention paid to the 16 simple rooms and to your needs.

🔒 E4 ✉ Via Faenza 89 ☎ 055 216 801; fax 055 212 039 🚌 4, 7, 10, 12, 13, 25, 31, 32, 33

PALAZZO RUSPOLI

www.palazzo-ruspoli.it
Ideally placed close to the Duomo and San Lorenzo, this 20-room hotel is an immaculate and comfortable place to stay with its attractive paintwork and patterned soft furnishings.

🔒 F5 ✉ Via de' Martelli 5 ☎ 055 267 0563; fax 055 267 0525 🚌 1, 6, 7, 11, 17

PORTA ROSSA

www.hotelportarossa.com
Good enough for Byron and Stendhal, this elegant, spacious hotel is in a 14th-century building close to the Ponte Vecchio and has 78 rooms. Facilities include a café and a billiard room.

🔒 F6 ✉ Via Porta Rossa 19 ☎ 055 287 551; fax 055 282 179 🚌 A

LA RESIDENZA

www.laresidenzahotel.com
Comfortable 23-room hotel on the top four floors of a 17th-century palazzo on the super-elegant Via de' Tornabuoni. A recent overhaul has resulted in some exceptionally well-appointed rooms with huge bathrooms. Rooms at the top have balconies and there is a small roof terrace. Friendly and considerate

owners ensure an enjoyable stay. Free Internet access is available.

🔒 E6 ✉ Via de' Tornabuoni 8 ☎ 055 218 684; fax 055 284 197 🚌 6, 11, 36, 37, A

RIVOLI

www.hotelrivoli.it
Close to Santa Maria Novella, the Rivoli is a beautifully renovated Franciscan monastery. The 69 rooms are simple with large marble bathrooms and some have a balcony or terrace.

🔒 E5 ✉ Via della Scala 33 ☎ 055278 61; fax 055 294 041 🚌 11, 36, 37, A

LA SCALETTA

www.lascaletta.com
For those who want to stay on the quieter south side of the river Arno, La Scaletta is in a peaceful spot close to Oltrano and the Boboli Gardens. The 14 rooms have a homey feel. Lovely terrace.

PRICING

Italian hotels are legally required to post rates for high and low season on the back of every bedroom door. You should agree on a price before making a reservation. Rates vary according to the season, sometimes by as much as 25 per cent. Some hotels charge the same rate year-round. Hotels often quote their most expensive rates. So if you want a particular hotel ask if they have a less-expensive room.

🔒 E7 ✉ Via de Guicciardini 13 ☎ 055 283 028; fax 055 289 562 🚌 D

TORNABUONI BEACCI

www.tornabuonihotels
Handsome hotel great for shopping and sightseeing. The large, leafy roof garden and antiques-filled lounge are quiet retreats from the frenzy outside on this busy street. The 40 bedrooms are simple and uncluttered, and each has its own private bathroom.

🔒 E6 ✉ Via de' Tornabuoni 3 ☎ 055 212 645; fax 055 283 594 🚌 6, 11, 36, A

VILLA FIESOLE

www.villafiesole.it
Located in the hilltop village of Fiesole, this hotel with 28 rooms, has an outdoor pool and a wonderful Victorian greenhouse that houses the breakfast room, a lounge area and several bedoooms. This hotel offers really good value for great surroundings.

🔒 Off map at M1 ✉ Via Beato Angelico 35 ☎ 055 597 252; fax 055 599 133 🚌 7

VILLANI

www.hotelvillani.it
Experience real value for the money at this 13-roomed hotel that attracts an interesting array of visitors, including Italian families. Situated close to the Duomo. Great views from the top floor terrace.

🔒 F5 ✉ Via delle Oche 11 ☎ 055 239 6451; fax 055 215 348 🚌 A

Luxury Hotels

PRICES

Expect to pay over €200 for a double room in a luxury hotel

BRUNELLESCHI

www.hotelbrunelleschi.it
A modern 96-room hotel housed in a medieval tower in a peaceful location just behind the Via Calzaiuoli.
🚇 F5 ✉ Piazza Santa Elisabetta 3 ☎ 055 27370; fax 055 219 653 🚌 A

EXCELSIOR

www.starwood.com
One of the grandest hotels in Florence, renowned for its old-fashioned opulence. Some of the 168 rooms have a view of the River Arno, and there is a roof terrace.
🚇 D5 ✉ Piazza Ognissanti 3 ☎ 055 271 51; fax 055 210 278 🚌 A, B

HELVETIA & BRISTOL

www.royaldemeure.com
An 18th-century hotel in a superb location near the Duomo. Each of the 67 rooms is decorated individually with rich furnishings, and some have antiques, too.
🚇 E5 ✉ Via dei Pescioni 2 ☎ 055 266 51; fax 055 288 353 🚌 6, 11, 36, 37, A

HERMITAGE

www.hermitagehotel.com
A well-known 29-room hotel overlooking the Ponte Vecchi, drawing visitors back time and time

again. Idyllic, light and airy roof garden.
🚇 F6 ✉ Vicolo Marzio 1, Piazza del Pesce ☎ 055 287 216; fax 055 212 208 🚌 B

HOTEL J & J

www.jandjhotelfirenze.com
Close to touristy Santa Croce, this is a quiet 20-room hotel in a 16th-century monastery, with a glamorous international clientele. Chic design.
🚇 H5 ✉ Via di Mezzo 20 ☎ 055 263 12; fax 055 240 282 🚌 C

KRAFT

www.krafthotel.it
Some of the 80 rooms are traditional, others are modern in this quiet and comfortable hotel, which also has a small roof-top swimming pool and some terrific views.
🚇 C5 ✉ Via Solferino 2 ☎ 055 284 273; fax 055 239 8267 🚌 B, D

PALAZZO MAGNANI FERONI

www.florencepalace.it
This is a grand place to stay by the side of the

LAST-MINUTE

If you arrive without a reservation, try the ITA (Informazioni Turistiche Alberghiere) office on the train station concourse (🕐 Daily 9–9 ☎ 055 282 893). You'll pay a fee of around €3–€8 for finding a room, depending on the category of hotel.

River Arno. It has an inner courtyard, vaulted ceilings and a lavish use of marble. The owners are very hospitable and will make all manner of arrangements for you. Twelve rooms in all.
🚇 D6 ✉ Borgo San Frediano 5 ☎ 055 239 9544; fax 055 260 8908 🚌 B, D

SAVOY

www.hotelsavoy.it
This 19th-century building in Piazza Della Republicca was reopened after massive renovation in 2000 and is now one of Florence's top boutique hotels. 102 sleek rooms.
🚇 F5 ✉ Piazza della Republicca 7 ☎ 055 27351; fax 055 273 588 🚌 A

VILLA CORA

www.villacora.it
A beautifully decorated 48-room villa with its own grounds overlooking the Oltrarno. Summer meals are served in the garden.
🚇 E9 ✉ Viale Machiavelli 18 ☎ 055 229 8451; fax 055 229 086 🚌 12, 13, 38

VILLA SAN MICHELE

www.villasanmichele.orient-express.com
Nestling in the Fiesole hills high above Florence this former monastery with 45 rooms offers the lushest of surroundings and the plushest of interiors and superb views. Very expensive.
🚇 Off map at M1 ✉ Via Doccia 4, Fiesole ☎ 055 567 8200; fax 055 567 8250 🚌 7

ORARIO CONTINUATO
8.00 – 20.00

FARMACIA

16 37

Florence is compact and the public transport good. Walking is probably one of the best and most rewarding ways of getting around. Petty crime is common but the city is relatively safe.

Need to Know

Planning Ahead

When to Go

Florence's peak season runs from February to October, although many consider it virtually uninterrupted. The city is overrun with tour groups in June and July. If you like heat, go in August—although many Florentines are on holiday and some restaurants close, it's a good time to go because everything is quieter.

> **TIME**
>
> Italy is one hour ahead of London, six hours ahead of New York and nine hours ahead of Los Angeles.

AVERAGE DAILY MAXIMUM TEMPERATURES											
JAN	FEB	MAR	APR	MAY	JUN	JUL	AUG	SEP	OCT	NOV	DEC
50°F	52°F	59°F	64°F	73°F	79°F	84°F	82°F	79°F	70°F	57°F	54°F
10°C	11°C	15°C	18°C	23°C	26°C	29°C	28°C	26°C	21°C	14°C	12°C

Spring (March to May) is a good time to visit if you want to avoid the summer heat.
Summer (June to August) can be extremely hot and humid, sometimes uncomfortably so in July and August.
Autumn (September to November) is generally the wettest time in Tuscany, and thunderstorms are common in September.
Winter (December to February) temperatures are often similar to those in northern European countries, and rainfall can be high.

WHAT'S ON

January *Pitti Immagine:* Fashion shows at the Fortezza da Basso.
February *Carnevale:* A low-key version of Venice's annual extravaganza.
March *Festa dell'Annunziata* (25 Mar): Traditionally the Florentine new year, with a fair to celebrate in Piazza Santissima Annunziata.
Scoppio del Carro: The Easter Sunday service at the Duomo culminates in an exploding carriage full of fireworks.
April *Mostra Mercato Internazionale dell' Artigianato:* An international arts and crafts festival in the Fortezza da Basso.
May *Maggio Musicale:* Florence's international music and dance festival.
Festa del Grillo (Sun after Ascension): Crickets are sold in cages, then released in the park of Le Cascine (▷ 98).
June *Calcio in Costume:* An elaborate football game between town districts played in medieval costume in Piazza Santa Croce (▷ 29); preceded by a procession.
Festa di San Giovanni (24 Jun): Fireworks are set off in Piazzale Michelangelo to celebrate the feast of the patron saint of Florence.
Estate Fiesolana (mid-Jun to Sep): A Fiesole arts festival.
September *Festa del Rificolona* (7 Sep): Children carry paper lanterns in Piazza Santissima Annunziata to honour the birth of the Virgin.
October *Amici della Musica* (Oct–Apr): Concerts. Tickets from Teatro della Pergola (☎ 055 226 4316).
November *Festival dei Popoli* (Nov–Dec): A film festival in the Palazzo dei Congressi, showing international films.

Useful Websites

www.enit.it
Florence is particularly well covered on the Italian Tourist Board website, with information on history, culture, events, accommodation and gastronomy, in several languages.

www.turismo.toscana.it
This site is run by the Tuscan Regional Tourist Board and covers the whole region as well as Florence, the capital.

www.comune.firenze.it
Florence City Council aims its website at locals, but its tourism, museum and art pages are always up-to-date, with some good links.

www.firenzeturismo.it
The official APT tourism site with plenty of useful information in English.

www.firenze.net
This Florence-based site, in Italian and English, has information on where to go and what to do, with good maps and plenty of links.

www.emmeti.it
Another Italy-based site, in Italian and English, with a good range of information and links for Florence. It is strong on local events and has an online hotel reservation service.

www.initaly.com
This lively US site is clearly run by passionate Italophiles and has excellent planning tips and sightseeing hints.

www.promhotels.it
Useful online hotel booking site for Florence and other Italian destinations.

www.florenceart.it
You can prereserve a timed entrance ticket, to avoid a long wait to the main Florentine museums including the Uffizi via this efficient site.

PRIME TRAVEL SITES

www.fodors.com
A complete travel-planning site. You can research prices and weather; book air tickets, cars and rooms; ask questions (and get answers) from fellow travellers; and find links to other sites.

www.trenitaliaplus.com
The official site of the Italian State Railways.

www.weatheronline.co.uk/Italy
Good three-day weather predictions.

INTERNET CAFÉS

Internet Train
www.internettrain.it
🚉 G5 ✉ Via dell' Orinolo 40r ☎ 055 263 8968;
🕐 Mon–Thu 10am–10.30pm, Fri, Sat 10–8, Sun 3–7
❓ Other branches in the city.

B–on line
🚉 G5 ✉ Via Sant' Egidio 37r ☎ 055 240 069; e-mail beonline@gmail.com
🕐 Daily 10.30–10.30

Into the Web
www.intotheweb.it
🚉 F5 ✉ Via de Conti 23r
☎ 055 264 5628;
🕐 10am–11pm ❓ Dell Pcs and Macs. Café.

Getting There

There are no direct intercontinental flights to Florence so visitors have to fly to Milan (298km/185 miles north), Rome (277km/172 miles south) or another European city, then take a connecting flight or train. The flight from New York to Rome takes around nine hours. From the airport, take a shuttle train to Stazione Termini, then a train to Florence (two hours).

For the latest passport and visa information, look up the British embassy website at www.britishembassy. gov.uk or the United States embassy at www.american embassy.com/europe

You can choose from three airports—Galileo Galilei Airport at Pisa, the small Amerigo Vespucci Airport at Florence and Guglielmo Marconi Airport at Bologna. The flight takes approximately 2 hours from London.

120KM (75 MILES)

Florence Airport
4km (2.5 miles) to central Florence
Bus, 20 minutes
€4

Bologna Airport
105km (65 miles) to Florence
Bus then train, 1 hour+
€14.50

Pisa Airport
91km (57 miles) to Florence
Train, 1 hour 15 minutes
€5.10

FROM FLORENCE AIRPORT

Amerigo Vespucci Airport (☎ 055 315 874; www.aeroporto.firenze.it), also known as La Peretola, is 4km (2.5 miles) northwest of the city. It handles mainly domestic flights, with a limited number of daily departures to other European cities. There are two terminal buildings. The airport is connected to Santa Maria Novella (SMN) station in Florence by blue SITA buses, which run every 30 minutes between 6am and 8.30pm, then every hour until 11.30pm. The journey takes 20 minutes and tickets, which cost €4, can be bought on board. The Vola In Bus runs to Piazza Adua (next to SMN) every 30 minutes between 6am and 11.30pm; cost €4. Taxis cost around €16, plus possible surcharges (always check and agree a price before you set off).

FROM PISA AIRPORT

Pisa's Galileo Galilei Airport (☎ 050 500 707; www.pisa-airport.com) is the region's main point of entry 91km (57 miles) west of Florence but with good road and train connections to the city. The one spacious terminal handles domestic and European flights. There are 8

trains a day leave for Florence between 6.40am and around 10.20pm. The journey takes about 75 minutes and costs €5.10. Additional trains leave from Pisa Centrale station, a 10-minute taxi ride away. Terravision runs an airport bus transfer, taking around 70 minutes, to Florence train station between 7.40am and 11.30pm, costing €7.50 one way, €13.50 return. A taxi to Florence costs around €129.

FROM BOLOGNA AIRPORT
Guglielmo Marconi Airport (☎ 051 647 9615; www.bologna-airport.it) is 105km (65 miles) northeast of Florence in the Emilia-Romagna region and handles a large volume of European charter and scheduled flights, as well as budget airline flights. A shuttle bus costing about €4.50 takes passengers to Bologna Centrale station. From here the journey takes about an hour and costs around €10, depending on type of train taken. Make sure the ticket is valid for the right train. Rental cars are available in Terminal A. A taxi to Florence costs about €200.

ARRIVING BY TRAIN
The main station, Santa Maria Novella, has links with major Italian cities as well as Paris, Ostend and Frankfurt. Most buses in Florence depart from the station forecourt, and there are usually taxis waiting. Don't forget to validate your ticket before boarding your train. Do this by inserting the ticket into the orange box on the platform.

ARRIVING BY LONG-DISTANCE BUS
Lazzi runs express services to and from Rome and links Florence with major European cities as part of the Eurolines network (✉ Piazza della Stazione 3r ☎ 055 363 041; www.lazzi.it).

CAR RENTAL
The major car rental groups are all represented in the region and have offices at airports, rail stations and in the bigger cities.

TRAVEL INSURANCE

Take out your insurance as soon as you book your trip to ensure you are covered for delays. Most policies cover cancellation, medical expenses, accident compensation, personal liability and loss of personal belongings (including money). Your policy should cover the cost of getting you home in case of medical emergency. An annual travel policy may be the best value if you intend to make several trips in a year away from home, but long trips abroad may not be covered. If you have private medical coverage, check your policy, as you may be covered while you are away.

NEED TO KNOW GETTING THERE

Getting Around

The Tuscan capital has no metro or subway system, but the historic part of the town is largely traffic-free and can be crossed on foot in 30 minutes. There are conventional bus services, but none of the routes are allowed to enter the traffic-free zone. These buses are useful, however, if you are staying on the outskirts of the city, or for getting around to the more outlying sights. In addition to the normal bus service there are four bus routes that do enter the traffic-free zone. Azienda Trasporti Area Fiorentina (ATAF) is responsible for public transportion in Florence (wwwataf.net).

BUSES

Bus routes in Florence are numbered and many start and end at the railway station at regular intervals (www.ataf.net). The zippy little electric buses that run through the traffice-free zone, identified by letters (A–D), link all kinds of places in the narrow streets of the old city. Buy tickets at bars and tobacconists before boarding. Once on board, insert your ticket into the small orange box and it will be stamped with the time. Failure to validate your ticket can result in a hefty fine. The ticket is valid for the next 60 minutes for any bus. The three-hour ticket works the same way as the 60-minute ticket but for three hours; a multiple ticket gives you four 60-minute tickets. The tourist information office by the station has bus maps.

HOP-ON-HOP-OFF BUS

If you really want to avoid any leg work, or want an overview of how the city is laid out, take an open-top bus ride with City Sightseeing (☎ 055 264 5363; www.city-sightseeing.it). This bus enables visitors to get on and off at any number of designated stops on the tourist itinerary. The ticket is valid for 24 hours and costs €20.

LONG-DISTANCE BUS

There are three main bus companies in Florence: **Lazzi** ✉ Piazza della Stazione 47 ☎ 055 363 041; www.lazzi.it

SITA serves the south and east region ✉ Via Santa Caterina da Siena 15r ☎ 055 219383; www.sita-on-line.it

CAP serves the region to the northeast of Florence, the Mugello ✉ Largo Fratelli Alinari 9 ☎ 055 214 637; www.capautolinee.it

TAXIS

Official Florentine taxis are comfortable, clean and white. You can hail them from central places such as the station or Piazza del Duomo, or call one of the official cab companies: Radio Taxi SO.CO.TA. (☎ 055 4798/4242) or Radio Taxi CO.TA.FI. (☎ 055 4390). The meter starts running the moment the call is received. Supplements are charged for baggage and for journeys at night.

BICYCLES AND MOTORCYCLES

Bicycles can be rented from Florence by Bike ✉ Via San Zanobi 120–122r ☎ 055 488 992 Mopeds and motorcycles can be rented from Alinari ✉ Via Guelfa 81r ☎ 055 280 500

CARS

It is really not worth driving around Florence. Much of the city is closed to traffic, there is a one-way system and parking is difficult. A car is ideal if you plan to tour the surrounding Tuscan countryside. If you do rent a car try to book a hotel with parking.

Car rental companies are in Borgo Ognissanti or Via Maso Finiguerra as follows:

Avis ✉ Borgo Ognissanti 128r ☎ 055 213 629
Hertz Italiana ✉ Via Finiguerra 33r ☎ 055 282 2260

Tuscany's road system ranges from motorways (expressways) to narrow winding lanes, and driving around outside the city is easy and a pleasure. Tolls are payable on highways (*autostrade*) and most fuel stations in the country now take credit cards, but by no means all.

Breakdown service: ✉ Viale G Amendola 36, Florence ☎ 116 or 055 24861

TIPS

● You should board a bus through the front or rear door, but exit through the middle ones.
● Children travel free if they are less than 1m (3.28ft) in height. Their height is checked against the box that you validate your ticket in.
● Smoking is not allowed on buses.
● A limited number of buses are adapted for passengers with disabilities.
● Bus routes are not always the same on the return leg so check the map at the bus stop to be sure you can get off at the stop of your choice.

NEED TO KNOW GETTING AROUND

119

Essential Facts

NEED TO KNOW ESSENTIAL FACTS

PRESS

● The Florentines preferred newspaper is *La Nazione*, a national paper produced in Florence.

● You can buy foreign newspapers and magazines at the station and at Sorbi (▷ 44), in Piazza della Signoria .

MONEY

The euro is the official currency of Italy. Bank notes in denominations of 5, 10, 20, 50, 100, 200 and 500 euros and coins in denominations of 1, 2, 5, 10, 20 and 50 cents and 1 and 2 euros were introduced on 1 January 2002.

10 euros

50 euros

200 euros

500 euros

ELECTRICITY

● Voltage is 220 volts and sockets take two round pins.

EMERGENCY TELEPHONE NUMBERS

● Police ☎ 113 Fire ☎ 115
● Ambulance ☎ 118
● Police headquarters ✉ Via Zara 2
☎ 055 49771

LOST PROPERTY

● Lost property office ✉ Via Circondaria 19
☎ 055 328 3942 ◑ 9–noon; closed Sun.
● Report losses of passports to the police and other items to the Questura at Via Zara 2
☎ 055 49771

MAIL

● Main post office ✉ Via Pellicceria 8 ☎ 055 27361 ◑ Mon–Fri 8.15–7, Sat 8.15–12.30.
● There is another big post office at ✉ Via Pietrapiana 53–55 ☎ 055 211 415 (same hours).
● Stamps (*francobolli*) can be bought from post offices or from tobacconists displaying a white T sign on a black or blue background.
● Post boxes are small, red and marked *Poste* or *Lettere*. The slot on the left is for addresses within the city and the slot on the right is for other destinations.

MEDICINES AND MEDICAL TREATMENT

● EU nationals receive reduced cost medical treatment on production of the relevant document (EHIC card for Britons). Private medical insurance for UK and all other nationals is still advised.
● Medical emergencies ☎ 118
● First aid: Misericordia ambulance service
☎ 055 212 222
● Tourist medical service: has English-speaking doctors on 24-hour call ✉ Via Lorenzo il Magnifico 59 ☎ 055 475 411
● Hospital: Santa Maria Nuova ✉ Piazza Santa Maria Nuova 1 ☎ 055 27581 Interpreters can

be arranged free through Associazione Volontari Ospedalieri ☎ 055 425 0126/234 4567

● Pharmacies are indicated by a large green or red cross.

● All-night pharmacies: Comunale 13 della Stazione ✉ At train station ☎ 055 216 761; All'insegna del Moro-Taverna ✉ Piazza San Giovanni 20r ☎ 055 211 343; Molteni ✉ Via dei Calzaiuoli 7r ☎ 055 289 490; Paglicci ✉ Via della Scala 61 ☎ 055 215 612

MONEY AND CREDIT CARDS

● American Express office ✉ Via Dante Alighieri 22r ☎ 055 50981
● Credit cards are widely accepted.
● Cash machines are now common.

NATIONAL HOLIDAYS

● 1 Jan: New Year's Day
● 6 Jan: Epiphany
● Easter Sunday
● Easter Monday
● 25 Apr: Liberation Day
● 1 May: Labour Day
● 15 Aug: Assumption
● 1 Nov: All Saints' Day
● 8 Dec: Immaculate Conception
● 25 Dec: Christmas Day
● 26 Dec: St. Stephen's Day.

CUSTOMS REGULATIONS

● EU nationals do not have to declare goods imported for their personal use.
● The limits for non-EU visitors are 200 cigarettes or 100 small cigars or 250g of tobacco; 1 litre of alcohol (over 22 per cent alcohol) or 2 litres of fortified wine; 50g of perfume.

TOILETS

● Italian toilets are improving both in cleanliness and facilities.
● Expect to pay about €0.25 for toilets . Those away from the main tourist areas are usually free.
● There are virtually no public toilets in Florence.
● Carry your own paper or at least a packet of tissues.
● Most bars and cafés have toilets, which usually allow anybody to use them (although it's polite to have at least a drink).

CONSULATES

British Consulate	✉ Lungarno Corsini 2 ☎ 055 284 133
US Consulate	✉ Lungarno Amerigo Vespucci 38 ☎ 055 266 951

PLACES OF WORSHIP

Anglican	St. Mark's BVia Maggio 16–18 ☎ 055 294 764
American Episcopal Church	St. James' ✉ Via Rucellai 9 ☎ 055 294 417
Lutheran	✉ Lungarno Torrigiani 11 ☎ 055 234 6343
Synagogue	✉ Via Farini 4 ☎ 055 245 252
Russian Orthodox	✉ Via Leone X 8 ☎ 055 490 148
Mosque	✉ Via Baaccio Bondinelli 11 ☎ 055 711 648

ETIQUETTE

● Make the effort to speak some Italian: It will be appreciated.

● Shake hands on introduction and on leaving; once you know people better you can replace this with a kiss on each cheek.

● Use the polite form, *lei*, unless the other person uses *tu*.

● Always say *buon giorno* (hello) and *arrivederci* (goodbye) in shops.

● Italians do not get drunk in public.

● Smoking is common everywhere.

PRECAUTIONS

● Take care of wallets, handbags and backpacks as pickpockets target tourists.

● Keep the receipts and numbers of your traveller's cheques separately from the traveller's cheques.

● Keep a copy of the front page of your passport.

● List the numbers and expiration dates of your credit cards and keep the list separately.

● If a theft occurs, make a statement (*denuncia*) at a police station within 24 hours if you wish to make an insurance claim.

● After dark avoid Le Cascine, Santa Maria Novella and the station.

OPENING TIMES

● Banks: 8.30–3; in some instances also 2.45–4 Mon–Fri.

● Post offices: Mon–Fri 8.15–1.30 Sat 8.15–12.30.

● Shops: normally 8.30–1 and from 3 or 4 until 7 or 8; or 10–7.

● Museums: see individual entries.

● Churches: 7 or 8–12.30 and then from between 3 and 4 until 7.30. Main tourist attractions often stay open longer. No two are the same.

TELEPHONES

● Public phones are orange. There is also a central office with a collection of phone booths (⊠ Via Cavour 21r ◷ Daily 8am–9.45pm).

● Few public telephones take coins. Phone cards (*carta* or *scheda* or *tessera telefonica*) are the most practical way to use a public phone.

● Directory Enquiries ☎ 12

● International directory enquiries ☎ 176 International operator ☎ 170; you can make reverse charge international calls by dialling 17200 followed by your country code (which will give you the operator).

● Cheap rate is all day Sunday and 9pm–8am (national) on other days; 10pm–8am (international).

● To call Italy from the UK, dial 00 followed by 39 (the code for Italy) then the number. To call the UK from Italy dial 00 44 then drop the first zero from the area code.

● To call Italy from the US dial 011 followed by 39. To call the US from Italy dial 00 1.

● Florence's area code (055) must always be dialled even if you are calling from within Florence.

TOURIST INFORMATION OFFICE

● Principal tourist office ⊠ Via Cavour 1r ☎ 055 290 832/3; fax 055 276 0383

Language

Italian pronunciation is totally consistent. Cs and gs are hard when they are followed by an *a*, *o* or *u* (as in 'cat' and 'got'), and soft if followed by an *e* or an *i* (as in 'child' or 'geranium').
The Tuscans often pronounce their *cs* and *chs* as *hs*.

USEFUL WORDS AND PHRASES

buon giorno	good morning
buona sera	good afternoon/ evening
buona notte	good night
ciao	hello/ goodbye (informal)
arrivederci	goodbye (informal)
arrivederla	goodbye (formal)
per favore	please
grazie	thank you
prego	you're welcome
come sta/stai?	how are you?
sto bene	I'm fine
mi dispiace	I'm sorry
scusi/scusa	excuse me/ I beg your pardon
permesso	excuse me (in a crowd)
quant'è?	how much is it?
quando?	when?
avete...?	do you have...?
qui/qua	here

BASIC VOCABULARY

sì	yes
no	no
non ho capito	I do not understand
sinistra	left
destra	right
entrata	entrance
uscita	exit
aperto	open
chiuso	closed
buono	good
cattivo	bad
grande	big
piccolo	small
con	with
senza	without
più	more

NUMBERS

uno/primo	1/first
due/secondo	2/second
tre/terzo	3/third
quattro/ quarto	4/fourth
cinque/quinto	5/fifth
sei	6
sette	7
otto	8
nove	9
dieci	10
venti	20
cinquanta	50
cento	100
mille	1,000
milione	1,000,000

EMERGENCIES

aiuto!	help!
dov'è il telefono più vicino?	where is the nearest telephone?
c'è stato un incidente	there has been an accident
chiamate la polizia	call the police
chiamate un medico/ un'ambulanza	call a doctor/an ambulance
pronto soccorso	first aid
dov'è l'ospedale più vicino?	where is the nearest hospital?

NEED TO KNOW TIMELINE

Timeline

THE FLORIN

Florence minted its own coins, florins, in silver in 1235 and in gold in 1252. Soon they were being used as the standard coin in Europe, evidence of the pre-eminence of Florence in European finance.

BEFORE 1000

Florence started to grow in 59bc as a result of an agrarian law passed by Julius Caesar, granting land to retired army veterans. Byzantine walls were added to the Roman walls in AD541–44, as protection against the Ostrogoths. The Lombards took Tuscany in 570 but were defeated in the early 9th century by Charlemagne. Florence became part of the Holy Roman Empire, ruled by imperial princes known as Margraves.

1115 The first comune (city state) is formed. Florence is run by a 100-strong assembly.

1250–60 The Primo Popolo regime controls Florence, dominated by trade guilds.

1296 The building of the Duomo begins, under Arnolfo di Cambio.

1340s Florence faces economic crisis after Edward III of England bankrupts the Peruzzi and Bardi and the Black Death plague halves the population.

1378 The uprising of the ciompi (wool carders) is the high point of workerunrest.

1406 Florence captures Pisa, gaining direct access to the sea.

1458 Cosimo de' Medici is recognized as ruler of Florence.

1469–92 Lorenzo the Magnificent rules.

1478 Pazzi conspirators plan to have Giuliano and Lorenzo murdered in the cathedral. Giuliano is killed but Lorenzo escapes.

1494 Florence surrenders to Charles VIII of France. Savonarola, a zealous monk, takes control of the city.

1498 Savonarola is burned at the stake after four years of rule, and Florence becomes a republic.

1502 The Republic of Florence retakes Pisa.

1570 Cosimo I creates a Tuscan state free from the Holy Roman Empire.

1743 Anna Maria Luisa, last of the Medici, dies. Florence is then ruled by the house of Lorraine under Francis Stephen.

1799–1814 Tuscany is occupied by Napoleon's troops.

1865–70 Florence becomes capital of Italy. King Vittorio Emanuele is installed in Pitti Palace.

1944 On 4 August, Germans blow up all the bridges in Florence except the Ponte Vecchio.

1966 The River Arno bursts its banks: Florence is flooded.

1993 The Uffizi Gallery is bombed.

2004 Michelangelo's *David* is unveiled in the Galleria dell'Accademia after controversial restoration.

2006 Florence Airport (Amerigo Vespucci) reopens in April after major renovation work.

FAMOUS FLORENTINES

The poet Dante Alighieri, author of the *Divine Comedy*, was born in Florence in 1265. He was exiled from the city in 1302 because of his sympathies with the White Guelphs, and died in 1321.

Michelangelo Buonarroti (1475–1564) created some of his most famous works in Florence, including the sculpture *David*. Born in Caprese, he was buried in Florence's Santa Croce.

Political philosopher Niccolò Machiavelli was born in Florence in 1469.

Galileo Galilei (1564– 1642), from Pisa, spent much of his life in Florence as the Medici court mathematician.

From far left: Bust of Cosimo di Giovanni de Medici and on his horse; Napoleon Bonaparte; Dante Alighieri; fleur-de-lys guild emblem; the defensive Forte di Belvedere

Index

Florence's
25 BEST

WRITTEN BY Susannah Perry
ADDITIONAL WRITING Jackie Staddon and Hilary Weston
DESIGN CONCEPT AND DESIGN WORK Kate Harling
INDEXER Marie Lorimer
EDITORIAL MANAGEMENT Apostrophe S Limited
REVIEWING EDITOR Jacinta O'Halloran
SERIES EDITOR Paul Mitchell

ISBN 978-1-4000-1761-4

SIXTH EDITION

IMPORTANT TIP
Time inevitably brings changes, so always confirm prices, travel facts, and other perishable information when it matters. Although Fodor's cannot accept responsibility for errors, you can use this guide in the confidence that we have taken every care to ensure its accuracy.

SPECIAL SALES
This book is available for special discounts for bulk purchases for sales promotions or premiums. Special editions, including personalized covers, excerpts of existing books, and corporate imprints, can be created in large quantities for special needs. For more information, write to Special Markets/Premium Sales, 1745 Broadway, MD 6–2, New York, NY 10019 or email specialmarkets@randomhouse.com.

First published 1997
Colour separation by Keenes
Printed and bound by Leo, China
10 9 8 7 6 5 4 3 2 1

A02815
Maps in this title produced from mapping © MAIRDUMONT / Falk Verlag 2006
Transport map © Communicarta Ltd, UK

The Automobile Association would like to thank the following photographers and companies for their assistance in the preparation of this book.

Abbreviations for the picture credits are as follows – (t) top; (b) bottom; (c) centre; (l) left; (r) right; (AA) AA World Travel Library

Inside front cover images: **1** AA/Simon McBride; **2** AA/Clive Sawyer; **3** AA/Simon McBride; **4** AA/Simon McBride; **5** AA/Simon McBride; **6** AA/Clive Sawyer; **7** AA/Clive Sawyer; **8** AA/Clive Sawyer; **9** AA/Terry Harris; **10** AA/Simon McBride

1 AA/Simon McBride; **2-18t** AA/Simon McBride; **4cl** AA/Simon McBride; **5c** AA/Ken Paterson; **6cl** AA/Simon McBride; **6cc** AA/Clive Sawyer; **6cr** AA/Simon McBride; **6bl** AA/Terry Harris; **6bc** AA/Ken Paterson; **6br** AA/Simon McBride; **7cl** AA/J Edmanson; **7cr** AA/Simon McBride; **7bl** AA/Clive Sawyer; **7br** AA/Simon McBride; **10ctr** AA/Simon McBride; **10cr** AA/Simon McBride; **10cbr** AA/Terry Harris; **10br** AA/Simon McBride; **11ctl** AA/Terry Harris; **11cbl** AA/Ken Paterson; **11bl** AA/Clive Sawyer; **13ctl** AA/Clive Sawyer; **13cl** AA/Terry Harris; **13cbl** AA/Clive Sawyer; **13bl** AA/Terry Harris; **14ctr** AA/Max Jourdan; **14cr** AA/Simon McBride; **14cbr** AA/Ken Paterson; **14br** AA/Terry Harris; **16ctr** AA/Simon McBride; **16cbr** AA/Ken Paterson; **16br** AA/Simon McBride; **17ctl** AA/Simon McBride; **17cl** AA/Simon McBride; **17cbl** AA/Clare Garcia; **17bl** AA/Terry Harris; **18ctr** AA/Clive Sawyer; **18cr** Photodisc; **18cbr** AA/Clive Sawyer; **18br** AA/Clive Sawyer; **19t** AA/Simon McBride; **19ct** AA/Ken Paterson; **19cb** AA/Richard Ireland; **19b** AA/Terry Harris; **20/21** AA/Clive Sawyer; **24l** AA/Clive Sawyer; **24/25t** AA/Clive Sawyer; **24/25c** AA/Simon McBride; **25tr** AA/J Edmanson; **25cl** AA/Ken Paterson; **25c** AA/Ken Paterson; **25cr** AA/Ken Paterson; **26l** AA/Simon McBride; **26r** Santa Croce, Florence, Giraudon/Bridgeman Art Library; **27l** AA/Simon McBride; **27r** AA/Clive Sawyer; **28l** AA/Simon McBride; **28c** AA/Simon McBride; **28r** AA/Simon McBride; **29l** AA/Clive Sawyer; **29r** Scala, Florence 2006; **30tl** AA; **30/31t** AA/Simon McBride; **30c** AA/Simon McBride; **30/31c** AA/Terry Harris; **31tr** AA/Simon McBride; **31cr** AA/Simon McBride; **32l** AA/Clive Sawyer; **32c** AA/Barrie Smith; **32r** AA/J Edmanson; **33** AA/Simon McBride; **34t** AA/Simon McBride; **34cl** AA/Terry Harris; **34c** AA/Clive Sawyer; **34cr** AA/Clive Sawyer; **35** AA/Terry Harris; **36l** AA/Clive Sawyer; **36c** AA/Terry Harris; **36r** AA/Clive Sawyer; **37-39t** AA/Ken Paterson; **37bl** AA/Ken Paterson; **37br** AA/Clive Sawyer; **38bl** AA/Clive Sawyer; **38br** AA/Clive Sawyer; **39bl** AA/Simon McBride; **39br** AA/Clive Sawyer; **40** AA/Terry Harris; **41t** AA/Terry Harris; **42t** AA/Simon McBride; **43t** AA/Simon McBride; **44t** AA/Simon McBride; **45t** AA/Simon McBride; **46t** AA/Terry Harris; **47t** AA/Eric Meacher; **48t** AA/Simon McBride; **49t** AA/Clive Sawyer; **50t** AA/Ken Paterson; **51** AA/Simon McBride; **54** AA/Clive Sawyer; **55** AA/Simon McBride; **56l** AA/Simon McBride; **56c** AA/Simon McBride; **56r** AA/Ken Paterson; **57l** AA/Terry Harris; **57r** AA/Terry Harris; **58tl** AA/Simon McBride; **58tr** AA/Clive Sawyer; **58cl** AA/Ken Paterson; **58cr** AA/Simon McBride; **59t** AA/Simon McBride; **59cl** AA/Simon McBride; **59cr** AA/J Edmanson; **60** Galleria dell' Accademia, Florence/Bridgeman Art Library; **60/61** Raffaello Bencini/Alinari Archives, Florence; **61r** AA/Simon McBride; **62l** AA/Simon McBride; **62r** AA/Simon McBride; **63l** AA/Simon McBride; **63r** AA/Simon McBride; **64l** AA/Terry Harris; **64r** AA/Terry Harris; **65l** AA/Simon McBride; **65r** AA/Simon McBride; **66l** AA/Simon McBride; **66c** AA/Clive Sawyer; **66r** AA/J Edmanson; **67l** AA/Clive Sawyer; **67r** AA/Terry Harris; **68-69t** AA/Terry Harris; **68b** AA/Simon McBride; **69bl** AA/Terry Harris; **69br** AA/Terry Harris; **70t** AA/Terry Harris; **71t** AA/Terry Harris; **72t** AA/Simon McBride; **73t** AA/Simon McBride; **74t** Digitalvision; **75t** AA/Simon McBride; **76t** AA/Terry Harris; **77** AA/Clive Sawyer; **80** AA/Simon McBride; **81** AA/Simon McBride; **82l** AA/Ken Paterson; **82r** AA/Clive Sawyer; **83l** AA/Clive Sawyer; **83r** AA/Simon McBride; **84t** AA/Simon McBride; **84c** AA/Richard Ireland; **84/85** AA/J Edmanson; **86-87t** AA/Ken Paterson; **86bl** AA/Simon McBride; **86br** AA/Clive Sawyer; **87b** AA/Simon McBride; **88t** AA/Terry Harris; **89t** AA/Ken Paterson; **90t** AA/Simon McBride; **91t** AA/Digitalvision; **91c** AA/Terry Harris; **92t** AA/Terry Harris; **93** AA/Terry Harris; **96** Seat Archive/Alinari Archives; **97** Museo Stibbert, Florence/Bridgeman Art Library; **98t** AA/Ken Paterson; **98b** AA/Clive Sawyer; **99t** AA/Ken Paterson; **99bl** AA/Terry Harris; **99br** AA/Terry Harris; **100t** AA/Ken Paterson; **100b** AA/Terry Harris; **101t** AA/Simon McBride; **102t** AA/Michelle Chaplow; **103t** Digitalvision; **104t** Photodisc; **105t** AA/Clive Sawyer; **106t** David Wasserman/brandxpictures; **107** AA/Clive Sawyer; **108-112t** AA/Clive Sawyer; **108ctr** AA/J Edmanson; **108cr** AA/Clive Sawyer; **108cbr** AA/Simon McBride; **108br** AA/Terry Harris; **113** AA/Terry Harris; **114-125t** AA/Terry Harris; **118b** AA/Terry Harris; **120** ECB; **124bl** AA; **124bc** AA/Clive Sawyer; **124bc** AA; **124br** AA/Clive Sawyer; **125bl** AA/Clive Sawyer; **125br** AA/Simon McBride.

Every effort has been made to trace the copyright holders, and we apologise in advance for any accidental errors. We would be happy to apply the corrections in the following edition of this publication.

p. 72

Frette
(fabrics)

2 Via
Cavour

Hotel Rivoli
Via della Scala 33
055-27861